ACCOUNTING DESK BOOK

The Accountant's Everyday Instant Answer Book

1997 Supplement

TENTH EDITION

TOM M. PLANK

PRENTICE HALL

Printed in the United States of America

10   9   8   7   6   5   4   3   2   1

This publication is designed to provide accurate and authoritative information in regard to the subject matter covered. It is sold with the understanding that the publisher is not engaged in rendering legal, accounting, or other professional service. If legal advice or other expert assistance is required, the services of a competent professional person should be sought.

. . . From the Declaration of Principles jointly adopted by a Committee of the American Bar Association and a Committee of Publishers and Associations.

ISBN   0-13-700196-7

ISSN   1090-039X

ATTENTION: CORPORATIONS AND SCHOOLS

Prentice Hall books are available at quantity discounts with bulk purchase for educational, business, or sales promotional use. For information, please write to: Prentice Hall Career & Personal Development Special Sales, 113 Sylvan Avenue, Englewood Cliffs, NJ 07632. Please supply: title of book, ISBN number, quantity, how the book will be used, date needed.

PRENTICE HALL
Career & Personal Development
Englewood Cliffs, NJ 07632
A Simon & Schuster Company

On the World Wide Web at http://www.phdirect.com

Prentice-Hall International (UK) Limited, *London*
Prentice-Hall of Australia Pty. Limited, *Sydney*
Prentice-Hall Canada Inc., *Toronto*
Prentice-Hall Hispanoamericana, S.A., *Mexico*
Prentice-Hall of India Private Limited, *New Delhi*
Prentice-Hall of Japan, *Tokyo*
Simon & Schuster Asia Pte. Ltd., *Singapore*
Editora Prentice-Hall do Brasil, Ltda., *Rio de Janeiro*

Contents

CHAPTER 2
DERIVATIVES: EVERYONE HAS AN OPINION   15

CHAPTER 3
IRAS, PENSION, AND ANNUITY INCOME   36

CHAPTER 6
FEDERAL TAX ASPECTS OF BANKRUPTCY **70**

CHAPTER 9
TRAVEL, ENTERTAINMENT, AND GIFT EXPENSES 108

CHAPTER 10
HOUSEHOLD EMPLOYER TAXES (NANNY TAX)   131

CHAPTER 11
THE SECURITIES AND EXCHANGE COMMISSION:
PRIVATE SECURITIES LITIGATION REFORM ACT OF 1995   134

About the Author

Tom M. Plank is a specialist in SEC Accounting Rules and Regulations, new security issues registration, and annual report filings with the SEC. He holds his degrees from the Graduate School of Management, University of California at Los Angeles.

Mr. Plank has served on the accounting and finance faculties of various major universities in Chicago and Los Angeles. His business experience includes that of an officer and economist for a large commercial bank, a securities analyst for an investment banking firm, an account executive and financial adviser for a large securities firm, and a consultant for various corporations.

Mr. Plank has published many articles in various journals and is the author of many books: *SEC Accounting Rules and Regulations, The Age of Automation, The Science of Leadership,* and more than five accounting books, including the seventh, eighth, ninth, and tenth editions with five supplements of the *Accounting Desk Book.*

How to Use This Supplement

The **objective** of this *Supplement* is to furnish users of the *Accounting Desk Book, Tenth Edition* — with the **latest** developments in the financial accounting rules. Most significant are Financial Accounting Standards Board Statements issued since the *Desk Book* was published, which govern the presentation of financial reports, and an update of federal tax regulations that are of significance to accountants and to financial officers of large and small business organizations. Among the topics featured in the *Supplement* are:

- Financial Accounting Standards Board Statements Nos. 120, 121, 122, 123, 124
- Derivatives and Hedging
- Overview of the Private Securities Litigation Act of 1995
- SEC Disclosure Simplification
- SEC Shelf Registration Requirements
- Nanny Tax Regulations
- Five Appendices:
    Securities and Exchange Commission Terminology
    Interest Netting
    Lobbying Expense
    Tip Income
    Proposed FASB Statements

The discussions throughout the *Supplement* are self-contained. References to text found in the *Accounting Desk Book, Tenth Edition*, are identified by *ADB*, followed by the chapter number where it can be found.

Supplement users will find the Index particularly helpful in locating all the major topics and minor subtopics that are covered in this Supplement.

Tom M. Plank

ACKNOWLEDGEMENTS

I would like to acknowledge the invaluable editorial assistance of Lois R. Plank, my wife, and Christie Anne Ciraulo, my daughter, both of whom are professional journalists.

Chapter 1

Five New Financial Accounting Standards Board Statements

ACCOUNTING AND REPORTING BY MUTUAL LIFE INSURANCE ENTERPRISES AND BY INSURANCE ENTERPRISES FOR CERTAIN LONG-DURATION PARTICIPATING CONTRACTS—FASB 120

FASB 120 is the result of considerable cooperation between the Financial Accounting Standards Board and the American Institute of CPAs to provide guidance in accounting, reporting, and disclosure procedures to mutual life insurance companies. Prior to the enactment of this standard and those rulings cited below, these companies reported financial information to their creditors and policyholders primarily following the statutory provisions of various state insurance regulatory bodies. The companies are now to report insurance and reinsurance activities according to GAAP.

The thrust of this Statement is to apply the provisions of FASB 60, *Accounting and Reporting by Insurance Enterprises*; FASB 97, *Accounting and Reporting by Insurance Enterprises for Certain Long-Duration Contracts and for Realized Gains and Losses from the Sale of Investments*, and FASB 113, *Accounting and Reporting for Reinsurance of Short-Duration and Long-Duration Contracts*, to mutual life insurance enterprises, assessment enterprises and to fraternal benefit societies. Certain participating life insurance contracts of those same enterprises have also been addressed in the AICPA's Statement of Position 95-1, *Accounting for Certain Activities of Mutual Life Insurance Enterprises*. Both become effective for financial statements for fiscal years beginning after December 15, 1995.

1

The three earlier FASB Statements had specifically exempted mutual life insurance enterprises from their requirements. FASB Interpretation 40, *Applicability of Generally Accepted Accounting Principles to Mutual Life Insurance and Other Enterprises*, did not address or change the exemption of mutual life insurance companies from these Statements. Interpretation 40 had been scheduled to become effective earlier but the date was changed to permit simultaneous application with FASB 120 and SOP 95-1.

It was because there seemed to be little authoritative accounting guidance relative to the insurance and reinsurance activities of Mutual Life Insurance Enterprises that the FASB, along with the AICPA, decided to extend the requirements of the above mentioned standards to them. The AICPA's Statement of Position 95-1 sets guidelines for participating insurance contracts of mutual life insurance companies when:

1) They are long-duration participating contracts that are expected to pay dividends to policyholders based on the actual experience of the insurer.
2) The annual policyholder dividends are paid in a way that identifies divisible surplus, then distributes that surplus in approximately the same proportion that the contracts are estimated to have contributed to that surplus. Otherwise, accounting and reporting for these contracts are covered by the (now) four basic FASB insurance enterprise standards listed above.

The effect of initially applying FASB 120 is to be reported retroactively through restatement of all previously issued annual financial statements presented for comparative purposes for fiscal years beginning after December 15, 1992. Annual statements filed prior to that date may also be restated for any desired number of consecutive annual periods. The cumulative effect of adopting FASB 120 is to be included in the earliest year restated.

ACCOUNTING FOR THE IMPAIRMENT OF LONG-LIVED ASSETS AND FOR LONG-LIVED ASSETS TO BE DISPOSED OF—FASB 121

FASB 121 sets up accounting standards for recording impairment of long-lived assets, certain identifiable intangibles, and goodwill applicable to assets which are to be held and used. In addition, it applies to those long-lived assets and certain identifiable intangibles which are to be disposed of. Statement 121 is effective for financial statements for fiscal years beginning after December 15, 1995, but the effects of the pronouncement have already become evident in companies that elected to comply with the provisions early and took major writedowns in the last quarter of 1995. Restatement of previously issued financial statements is not permitted.

FASB 121 does *not* apply to accounting for assets which are already covered by the following Statements:

1) FASB 50, *Financial Reporting in the Record and Music Industry,*
2) FASB 53, *Financial Reporting by Producers and Distributors of Motion Picture Films,*
3) FASB 63, *Financial Reporting by Broadcasters,*
4) FASB 86, *Accounting for the Costs of Computer Software to be Sold, Leased, or Otherwise Marketed,* and by
5) FASB 90, *Regulated Enterprises—Accounting for Abandonments and Disallowances of Plant Costs.*

Additionally, FASB 121 does not cover mortgage and related servicing rights, deferred tax assets, deferred policy acquisition costs, financial instruments, or certain long-term customer relations of financial institutions. The term *asset* within the scope of this Statement refers to assets grouped together at the lowest level at which cash flows can be identified and be relatively independent of the cash flows of other groups of assets.

Impairment Review

The basic requirement is that the *assets being held and used* by an entity must be reviewed for impairment whenever there is any indication that the carrying amount of the particular asset might not be recoverable.

Events or changes which could signal the time for a review for impairment include the following:

1) Significant reduction in the usefulness of the asset.
2) Significant alteration in the way in which an asset is used to the detriment of its value.
3) Significant reduction in the market value of the asset.
4) Adverse change in the general business climate that could affect the value of an asset.
5) Adverse change in the laws or regulations relating to the asset.
6) Continued operating or cash flow loss.
7) Forecasted continuing losses or lack of long-term profitability related to a supposedly revenue-producing asset.
8) Costs exceeding those anticipated for the acquisition or construction of an asset.
9) Significant change in the physical condition of an asset.
10) Adverse legal or regulatory action against the asset.

As noted above, the basic tenet of this Statement is that assets should be reported at their recoverable amounts. If circumstances such as those listed above appear to have occurred to the extent that the carrying amount of a particular asset may, in fact, not be recoverable, a review for impairment is required. The thinking behind these provisions is that a tangible or intangible asset or group of assets, including goodwill, is impaired when the book value is not recoverable. Impairment is measured by the projected cumulative, undiscounted cash flow (excluding interest charges) related to the asset. If the resulting total amount for estimated future cash flows from the use of the asset and eventual disposition is less than the carrying amount, FASB 121 mandates that a new, lower cost basis for the asset be established. For those long-lived assets and identifiable intangibles an entity plans to hold and use, the new cost basis is to be set at fair value. The writedown is to be charged to income as an impairment loss.

For a depreciable asset, the new lower cost is to be depreciated over the remaining useful life of that asset. Whether there has actually been an impairment loss or not, when need for a review has been signaled, this might also be an appropriate time for a review of depreciation policies in line with APB 20, *Accounting Changes*.

The FASB decided that an impairment loss cannot be considered similar to an extraordinary item or a loss from discontinued operations. Thus, impairment losses are to be classified as components of earnings (losses) from continuing operations.

If an asset being assessed for possible impairment was acquired in a business combination and accounted for using the purchase method, any goodwill included must be considered in the asset grouping and pro rated appropriately.

When goodwill *is* included as a portion of the impairment of a particular asset group, the carrying value of the goodwill must be eliminated prior to reducing the carrying value of impaired long-lived assets and other identifiable intangibles to the current fair value. As a result of this provision, it is probable that if a company appears to have overpaid for an acquisition because it is not producing the anticipated level of positive cash flow, the company will have decided to take a look down the road and write off the related goodwill.

This new Statement requires that the long-lived assets and certain identifiable intangibles which are *being disposed of* must be reported at the lower of carrying amount or fair value less the cost to sell the asset except when covered by APB-30, *Reporting the Results of Operations—Reporting the Effects of Disposal of a Segment of a Business, and Extraordinary, Unusual and Infrequently Occurring Events and Transactions*. These assets will still be reported at the carrying amount or net realizable value, less the cost to sell the asset, whichever is lower.

The Statement also requires that a rate regulated entity must recognize an impairment when a regulator excludes all or a part of a cost from the entity's rate base.

The initial application of FASB 121 to assets being held at the time of adoption are to be reported as the cumulative effect of a change in accounting principle as prescribed in APB 20.

As stated above, in measuring for possible impairment, the use of the term *asset* here refers to assets grouped together at the lowest level at which cash flows can be identified and are relatively independent of cash flows of other groups of assets. Obviously, the formation of these groupings can lead to very subjective decisions. Differing businesses and industries operating under varying circumstances and conditions could conceivably justify disparate groupings. Decisions relating to grouping, as well as to estimating expected cash flow, must give due concern to possible outcomes and be founded on carefully considered facts, assumptions, and projections.

Unlike the accounting standards established in many countries and proposed by the International Accounting Standards Committee, this measure does not permit the write-back of impaired asset values from previous writedowns or writeoffs.

Fair value in the context of FASB 121 refers to the amount at which an asset could be exchanged in a current transaction between willing parties—not in a forced or liquidation sale. Determining the fair value of an asset is guided by several considerations:

1) The best indication would be the sales price or bid/asked price of that or a similar asset obtained from a securities exchange registered with the SEC; or an over-the-counter quotation if reported by NASDAQ or the National Quotation Bureau; or a foreign market price if that market is comparable to a U.S. exchange or market.

2) Otherwise, the estimate must be based on fundamental analysis employing whatever reliable information and valuation techniques are available: price of similar assets, appraisals, present value of estimated cash flows discounted for risk, option-pricing models, matrix pricing, and option-adjusted spread models, for example.

Impairment losses for assets being held and used in operations are to be reported as a component of income from continuing operations before income taxes in the income statement (for-profit entities) or in the statement of activities (not-for-profit organizations).

Reporting and Disclosure

Disclosures to be made in the financial statements of the periods covering any impairment writedowns for assets to be held and used include the following:

1) A description of the impaired assets and the facts and circumstances leading up to recognition of impairment.

2) The extent of impairment and the methods used in determining the fair value.

3) The specific entry in the income statement or the statement of activities where the amount is reported, whether as a separate line item or part of an aggregated entry.

4) The segments affected, if applicable.

Financial statement reporting and disclosure requirements for assets to be disposed of include:

1) A description of the assets targeted for disposal, facts and circumstances leading up to the planned disposal, the expected disposal date, and the carrying amount of the targeted assets.

2) The business segment in which assets to be disposed of are located.

3) Any impairment loss resulting from the initial measurement made at the time of the decision to dispose of the asset.

4) Any gain or loss resulting from changes in the carrying amount of assets to be disposed of.

5) Identification of the entry in the income statement or statement of activities in which any gains or losses are aggregated if they were not pre sented as a separate entry or reported on the face of the statement.

6) The results of operations for those assets to the extent the results are included in the entity's results of operations for the period and are identifiable.

Accounting for Real Estate

This standard is expected to have particular importance in bringing about accounting changes for companies with substantial real estate holdings. When these companies adopt the requirements, many will probably take significant writedowns whether their real estate assets are for rental to outsiders or for internal use. This group will include not only home builders who still hold high-priced land acquired during the 1980 boom years, but also owners of office buildings, shopping centers, apartment buildings, and hotels being carried at inflated prices.

FASB 121 could also cause substantial writedowns by companies with long-lived assets, which could impact the companies' earnings and share values. As mentioned elsewhere, however, the companies that take these writedowns could increase future earnings and also reduce future depreciation charges.

Accounting requirements previously had real estate companies carry for-sale real estate inventory at the lower of cost or net realizable value which places an asset at a value where it will break even in the future. Under the new standard, if a valuation adjustment is required, the asset is written down instead to fair value. This is usually a considerably more conservative measurement than net realizable value.

Accounting standards have been vague enough in the valuation of real estate held for use in the business that some companies have carried assets at depreciated cost with no writedowns even when returns on the assets were negative. Now assets held for use must be carried at the lower of their carrying values or fair value, but only if they fail an impairment test where the sum of the undiscounted cash flows before interest is less that the carrying amounts.

Real estate developers who issue financial statements will find specific instructions in FASB 121 for evaluating the impairment of real estate projects premised upon whether:

1) They are being held for and/or are in the process of development, or
2) They are substantially completed and ready for their intended use.

In effect, this new standard amends the impairment criteria established in FASB 67, *Accounting for Costs and Initial Rental Operations of Real Estate Projects.*

Projects held for development and sale are to be checked for impairment following the recognition and measurement provisions covering assets to be held and used. Thus, property that is being held for development, and property which is presently under development but not yet completed, should be checked for impairment only if events or changing circumstances signal possible impairment. If the estimated, undiscounted cash flows from the project fall short of the recorded cost, the property must be written down to fair value.

On the other hand, projects that are substantially completed and ready for sale or rental are to be accounted for as assets to be disposed of, and must be reported at the lower of carrying amount or fair value less cost to sell, except as mentioned above when covered by APB 30.

Specific indicators for real estate owners and developers that impairment may exist would include:

1) Expiration of material leases.
2) Insufficient rental demand for a project under development.
3) Deterioration of an area in which rental or sales property is located

Overall Effect

Insofar as company balance sheets are concerned, this Statement should result in the presentation of a more realistic picture of the value of an entity's assets. Since a company can no longer offset assets against each other, the impaired assets must be written off. Thus, current profit will be reduced when the one-time asset impairment charges are recorded. The financial picture after the writedown will show lower future costs resulting in higher future profits. Cash flow will not be affected by the writedown.

This improving financial picture may not necessarily mean that the future profit increases are the result of improving operations, only that "dead wood" has been trimmed from the balance sheet. On the other hand, the need to take a closer look at operations may very well lead to greater efficiency and improved capital allocation leading to increased economic value.

Part of the impetus for the adoption of this Statement was an attempt to increase the usefulness of financial reporting by making a comparison of entities with impairment losses more readily available. It is the belief of the majority of the FASB members that it will now be easier for financial statement users to compare one entity's response to economic or other outside forces to another entity's response to the same situation.

This Statement brings a greater degree of uniformity to financial reporting by providing accounting guidelines on when to test long-lived assets for impairment and how to go about the calculation. However, as in many prescribed situations, much is left to the discretion of management. The timing of the recognition of impairment, the measurement of the losses, the discount rate to use for similar levels of risk, and the composition of *asset groups* are examples of elements that may justifiably vary.

ACCOUNTING FOR MORTGAGE SERVICING RIGHTS—FASB 122

FASB 122 is an amendment to FASB 65, *Accounting for Certain Mortgage Banking Activities*. Mortgage servicing organizations often acquire the rights to service loans for others for a fee by purchasing or originating loans. They may then turn around and sell the loans, but keep the rights to service them.

FASB 65 made a distinction between loans originated by the servicer and those purchased. As a result, different accounting treatment was given to similar assets. To correct this situation, FASB 122 requires that mortgage service organizations recognize as separate assets the rights to service loans regardless of the manner in which they were acquired.

Change of Direction

In effect, this means an about face in GAAP from a prohibition against to a mandatory requirement to capitalize the cost of originating mortgage servicing rights when:

1) There is a definitive plan to sell or securitize the related mortgages.
2) The fair value of the mortgage and related servicing rights can be measured.

Accounting for the cost of mortgage servicing rights is to be handled in the following manner regardless of where and how the costs originated:

1) Cost of acquisition includes the cost of related mortgage servicing rights.

2) When a mortgage banking enterprise sells or securitizes a mortgage but retains servicing rights, total cost of the mortgage loan should be allocated to the mortgage servicing rights and the loans (minus the mortgage servicing rights) based on the fair values of each.

3) If there appears to be no practicable way to determine the fair values of each, the total cost of acquisition is to be allocated to the loan only with no cost being allocated to the servicing rights.

4) Any cost allocated to servicing rights constitutes a separate asset.

5) Mortgage servicing rights are to be amortized in proportion to and covering the period of their net servicing income.

6) Mortgage servicing rights are to be evaluated for impairment based on their fair value. In addition to the usual guidance provided for determining fair value (refer to discussion of FASB 121 above), other suggestions for determining fair value and measuring for impairment with specific attention to mortgage servicing rights are mentioned in the provisions in FASB 122.

Precautions

Among the "flags" to keep in mind are:

1) Mortgage servicing rights are subject to devaluation resulting from prepayment of loans.

2) During an economic downturn, borrowers may find it necessary to default on loans.

3) When interest rates drop, borrowers will refinance to take advantage of the lower rates.

4) The predominant risk characteristics of different types of loans, such as various conventional or government guaranteed or insured mortgaged loans and adjustable-rate or fixed-rate loans, must be considered.

5) Factors relating to loan size, note rate, date of origination, term, and geographic location are relevant.

To put it succinctly, no matter how mortgage servicing rights were acquired, this new Statement requires mortgage servicers to recognize them as separate assets.

Sections of the Statement include background information, benefits and costs, recognition and measurement, recognition of gains on sales of mortgage loans, and other aspects of mortgage servicing.

FASB 122 applies prospectively beginning after December 15, 1995.

The costs associated with retained servicing rights generated internally must be capitalized. Growth companies that retain these rights may very well find that they benefit from FASB 122's provisions.

ACCOUNTING FOR STOCK-BASED COMPENSATION—FASB 123

Passage of FASB 123 is not so much a compromise measure as an apparent agreement to get on to something else. In the final (for the time being) analysis, it offers an alternative approach to the present method of using APB Opinion 25, *Accounting for Stock Issued to Employees*, to account for stock options.

The new Statement sets forth a preferred method for accounting for stock based employee compensation; however, companies are not required to follow the new guidelines, but may continue in their present accounting practice with only slight modification. The alternative approaches are:

1) The fair value method.
2) The intrinsic value method.

Fair Value Method

In line with the current effort to bring a greater degree of uniformity and understanding to financial reporting, the FASB has premised the preferred method on fair value. Using this procedure, stock-based compensation cost is measured at the grant date based on the value of the award and is recognized over the employee's entire service period which is also normally the vesting period.

For stock options granted by a public entity, the fair value is determined using an option-pricing model that considers several factors present on the grant date—the exercise price and expected life of the option, the current price of the underlying stock and its expected volatility, expected dividends on the stock with specified exception, and the risk-free interest rate for the expected term of the option. The text suggests the Black-Scholes or a binomial model. When the fair value of the option has been determined at the grant date, it is not later adjusted for changes in the price of the underlying stock, its volatility, the life of the option, dividends on the stock or for the risk-free interest rate. For a nonpublic enterprise, the procedure is the same except that expected volatility need not be considered in estimating the option's fair value. Exclusion of the volatility factor in the estimation results in what is termed *minimum value*.

The Board feels that it should be possible to reach a reasonably accurate estimate of the fair value of most stock options and other equity instruments when they are granted. However, if there are complicated features which make this extremely difficult, even impossible, alternatives are suggested. If all else fails in finding a satisfactory estimate for the grant date, the Statement provides that the final measure of compensation cost is to be the value based on the stock price and any other pertinent information available on the first date that it *is possible* to reach a reasonable estimate of the value—generally, the date when the number of shares to which an employee is entitled and the exercise price are both determinable.

For nonvested or restricted stock awarded to an employee, the fair value is measured at the market price—or estimated market price if the stock is not publicly traded—of a share of nonrestricted stock at the grant date.

Intrinsic Value Method

Stock-based compensation standards have heretofore been based on APB 25, and probably will continue to be so for most companies. Using the intrinsic value method, compensation cost is the excess, if there is any, of the quoted market price of the particular stock over the employee's exercise price at the grant date or at another specified measurement date—perhaps the service date.

There actually is no intrinsic value or excess of exercise price over market price of the stock at the grant date for most fixed stock option plans. Therefore, these current accounting requirements generally do not result in an expense charge for most options. Therefore, no compensation cost is recognized. On the other hand, normally a compensation cost is recognized for other types of stock compensation plans under the intrinsic value method. They are usually plans with variable, often performance-based features.

Exceptions

Compensation costs need not be recognized for employee stock purchase plan discounts under the new Statement if the following three conditions exist:

1) The discount is relatively small.
2) Substantially all full-time employees participate on an equitable basis.
3) Provisions in the plan do not include any stock option features.

The compensation cost of stock awards required to be settled in cash is the amount of the change in the stock price in the periods in which the changes occur.

Additional Requirements

While FASB 123 is effective for calendar year 1996 and information about options granted in 1995 must be included in the 1996 financial statements, the decade-long consideration of the controversial issue only "encourages" companies to account for stock compensation awards based on their fair value at the date the awards are granted with the compensation cost shown as an expense on the income statement.

Companies continuing to use the APB 25 intrinsic value method will be required to disclose, but only in a note to the financial statements, what the net income and earnings would have been had they followed the new accounting method.

Controversy

The Board had long hoped to require full-scale fair value type measurement and accounting for employee stock compensation using a generally accepted options pricing model; however, those outside the Board were not ready to accept a mandate. After rather overwhelming pressure for more than a year from Congress, other politicians, other government agencies, business, and CPAs in public practice as well as those with commercial and industrial companies, a majority of the Board decided to emphasize improving disclosure rather than holding out for requiring an expense charge for all options.

ACCOUNTING FOR CERTAIN INVESTMENTS HELD BY NOT-FOR-PROFIT ORGANIZATIONS—FASB 124

FASB 124 is another step in the process of bringing reason, conformity, consistency, and comparability in accounting and financial reporting to the world of not-for-profit entities.

Earlier measures include:

1) FASB 93, *Recognition of Depreciation by Not-for-Profit Organizations.*
2) FASB 116, *Accounting for Contributions Received and Contributions Made.*
3) FASB 117, *Financial Statements of Not-for-Profit Organizations.* (See discussions in *ADB*, Chapter 13.)

This latest statement is reminiscent of FASB 115, *Accounting for Certain Investments in Debt and Equity Securities*, to the extent that it covers the same securities; however, accounting treatment for NPOs is markedly different from that applied to for-profit businesses.

Fair Value Requirements

Statement 124 requires that certain equity securities and all investments in debt securities be reported at fair value. The specific equity securities are those with readily determined fair value which are not accounted for by the equity method or as investments in consolidated subsidiaries. Gains and losses are to be reported in the statement of activities. This Statement also requires specific disclosures about all investments including the return on the investments.

Readily determinable fair value of an equity security is considered to have been met if one of the following criteria applies:

1) Sale prices or bid or asked quotations are available on an SEC registered exchange.
2) Sales prices or bid or asked prices on OTC markets or if they are reported by NASDAQ or the National Quotation Bureau.
3) If the equity security is traded only on a foreign market, that market is comparable to one of those given above.
4) If a mutual fund investment, fair value per share or unit has been determined and published as the basis for ongoing transactions.

Although many NPOs have been reporting all of their investments at fair value, it has not been required; therefore, there has been a considerable degree of diversity in the various organizations' accounting and financial reporting. The FASB believes that fair value will give a truer picture of the resources available for the further growth of the program of a not-for-profit organization. In addition, not only the staff and administrators, but also the donors will have improved information to assist them in allocating their efforts and resources.

Accounting Procedures

Application of this Statement may be made in either of two ways:

1) Restating of all financial statements presented for prior years.
2) Recognizing the cumulative effect of the change in the year of adoption.

Accounting and reporting for investments by various types of not-for-profit organizations has heretofore been provided by several AICPA guides. Any guidance in those sources which is inconsistent with the provisions of FASB 124 are superseded by these new requirements in this Statement.

In addition to the accounting principles set forth in this pronouncement, any additional disclosure requirements not discussed here but included in three previous Statements do apply to investments held by not-for-profit entities as well as to for-profit companies. The three are:

1) FASB 105, *Disclosure of Information about Financial Instruments with Off-Balance Sheet Risk and Financial Instruments with Concentrations of Credit Risk.*
2) FASB 107, *Disclosure about Fair Value of Financial Instruments.*
3) FASB 119, *Disclosure about Derivative Financial Instruments and Fair Value of Financial Instruments.*

(These Statements are also discussed in *ADB*, Chapter 10.)

Disclosure and Reporting

The Statement of Activities for each reporting period for an NPO must include the following specific items:

1) Investment income from dividends, interest, etc.
2) Net gains or losses on investments reported at other than fair value.
3) Net gains or losses on those reported at fair value.
4) Reconciliation of investment return if separated into operating and non-operating amounts.
5) Description of the policy used to decide what items should be included in determining operating costs.
6) Discussion for so doing if there is a change in that policy.

The Statement of Financial Position for each reporting period for an NPO must include the following:

1) Aggregate carrying amount of investments by major type.
2) Basis on which carrying amounts were determined for investments other than equity securities with readily determinable fair value and all debt securities.
3) Procedures used in determining fair values of investments other than financial instruments if carried at fair value. (Financial instruments are covered by the same requirement in FASB 107.)
4) Aggregate amount of any deficiencies in donor-related funds in which fair value of the assets has fallen below the level necessary to abide by donor stipulation or legal requirements.

For the most recent period, a not-for-profit organization must disclose in the Statement of Financial Position the nature of and carrying amount of any investments that represent a significant concentration of market risk.

Chapter 2
Derivatives: Everyone Has an Opinion

There is little doubt that Derivatives is the '90s buzz word in the areas of accounting, finance, banking, and investments. The SEC, the AICPA, the FASB, the GASB, the GAO, the FEI, the AIMR, the IASC, IOSCO, and myriad other worthy organizations have all jumped into the fray to attempt to prevent another Orange County, California-type debacle from occurring. The losses of Procter and Gamble, other large companies, and banks had raised concern, but the fiasco of a public body so obviously misusing derivatives—and being caught—called for drastic action. How best to guard against anything like this happening again?

At this juncture, all of the above named agencies and organizations appear to have reached the stage of agreeing to disagree, but amicably. All have taken important steps in attempts to ameliorate the ills and emphasize the positive uses of derivatives. Most have also suggested how some other group should do such and such to attack the problems.

The Financial Accounting Standard Board's FASB 119, *Disclosure About Derivative Financial Instruments and Fair Value of Financial Instruments*, was a giant step in the right direction as far as disclosure was concerned. (See *ADB* Chapter 10.) In addition, the FASB is currently working on at least two additional Statements relating to derivatives—one on hedging and the other a more comprehensive accounting for derivatives.

Various private sector entities have highlighted, pinpointed, and underlined problems associated with disclosures about these market risk sensitive instruments, as identified by users of financial reports. The Securities and Exchange Commission's study, preceding the release (in March, 1996) of their proposals for amendments to regulations governing disclosure information about derivatives and other financial instruments, took into consideration concerns by many organizations. For example, the Association for Investment Management and Research (AIMR), an organization of financial analysts, in a paper discussing financial reporting in the 1990s and on into the next century noted that users are confounded by the complexity of financial instruments.

After considerable investigation into the needs of investors and creditors, the American Institute of Certified Public Accountants' (AICPA) Special Committee on Financial Reporting confirmed in a study completed in 1994 that users are confused. The users complained that business reporting is not meeting their needs in answering difficult but important questions about innovative financial instruments that companies may have entered into. They felt they needed more specific information about how companies account for those instruments, how that accounting affects the financial statements, and how risk is handled.

Other organizations have recently made recommendations about how to improve such disclosures on market risk sensitive instruments. These organizations include regulators, such as the Group of Ten Central Bankers, the Federal Reserve Bank of New York, the Basle Committee and the Technical Committee of the International Organization of Securities Commissions (lOSCO), and private sector bodies, such as the Group of Thirty and a task force of the Financial Executives Institute (FEI).

The SEC study found that, in general, these organizations have stressed the need to make more understandable the risks inherent in market risk sensitive instruments. In particular, they have called for additional quantitative and qualitative disclosures about market risk. For example, the Federal Reserve Bank of New York recommended a new financial statement providing quantitative information about the overall market risk of an entity. In addition, the FEI task force recommended that companies disclose some type of information that conveys overall exposure to market risk. In this regard, the FEI task force suggested two distinct approaches. One approach is to provide a high-level summary of relevant statistics about outstanding activity at period end. The second approach is to communicate the potential loss which could occur under specified conditions using either a value at risk or another comprehensive model to measure market risk. (See the discussion of the U.S. General Accounting Office study and suggestions on derivative regulation below.)

SECURITIES AND EXCHANGE COMMISSION STUDY

At this juncture, it appears that the Securities and Exchange Commission is the body taking the most aggressive steps toward actual implementation of additional safeguards for derivative dealings. Inasmuch as the SEC is taking the view that much of the "derivative problem" can at least be alleviated by an improved financial statement and the accounting thereto, the prudent accountant might do well to become thoroughly aware of the direction in which the SEC seems to be going and the thinking behind the proposals. Much of the remedial effort will certainly become the responsibility of the accountant.

FASB Statement 119, The First Step

FASB 119 prescribes, among other things, disclosures in the financial statements about the policies used to account for derivative financial instruments and a discussion of the nature, terms, and cash requirements of derivative financial instruments. It also encourages, but does not require, disclosure of quantitative information about an entity's overall market risk. As mentioned earlier, this was a first decisive step in the right direction, but further standards have not as yet been finalized. (See the discussion of Proposed FASB Statements in Appendix E.)

During 1994, in response, in part, to the concerns of investors, regulators, and private sector entities, the SEC staff reviewed the annual reports of approximately 500 registrants. In addition, during 1995, more recent annual reports were reviewed by the SEC staff to assess the effect of FASB 119 on disclosures about market risk sensitive instruments. As a result of these reviews, the SEC staff observed that FASB 119 did have a positive effect on the quality of disclosures about derivative financial instruments. However, the SEC staff also concluded there was a need to improve disclosures about them, other financial instruments, and derivative commodity instruments. In particular, the SEC staff identified the following three primary disclosure issues.

Further Disclosure Measures Needed

1) Footnote disclosures of accounting policies for derivatives often are too general to convey adequately the diversity in accounting that exists for derivatives. As a result, it is often difficult to determine the impact of derivatives on registrants' statements of financial position, cash flows, and results of operations.

2) Disclosures frequently focus on derivatives and other financial instruments only in isolation. For this reason, it may be difficult to assess whether these instruments increase or decrease the net market risk exposure of a registrant.

3) Disclosure about financial instruments, commodity positions, firm commitments, and other anticipated transactions, *reported items*, in the footnotes to the financial statements, Management's Discussion and

Analysis (MD&A), schedules, and selected financial data may not reflect adequately the effect of derivatives on such reported items. Without disclosure about the effects of derivatives, information about the reported items may be incomplete or perhaps misleading.

FOR STUDY AND CONSIDERATION

For one and one-half years, members of the SEC staff researched derivatives, related risk management activities, and alternative disclosure approaches to make these activities less a mystery to investors, the general public, and even many professionals who actually deal with these activities in one capacity or another, before drawing up proposals for consideration. In addition, during this period, the SEC and its staff developed a list of guiding principles to provide a foundation for proposed amendments and recommendations.

1) Disclosures should make it possible for investors to understand better how derivatives affect a registrant's statements of financial position, cash flows, and results of operations.
2) Disclosures should provide information about market risk.
3) Disclosures should clearly explain for the investor how market risk sensitive instruments are used in the registrant's business.
4) Disclosures about market risk should not focus on derivatives in isolation, but rather should point out the "opportunity" for loss inherent in all market risk sensitive instruments.
5) Disclosure requirements about market risk should be flexible enough to accommodate different types of registrants, different degrees of market risk exposure, and different ways of measuring market risk.
6) Disclosures about market risk should highlight, where appropriate, special risks relating to leverage, option, or prepayment features.
7) New disclosure requirements should build on existing disclosure requirements, where possible, to simplify the learning process for additional procedures and to minimize compliance costs to registrants.

DERIVATIVES—GOOD AND BAD

During the last several years, there has been substantial growth in the use of derivative financial instruments, other financial instruments, and derivative commodity instruments. The SEC agrees that these instruments can be effective tools for managing registrants' exposures to market risk. After all, grain futures, hedging, and the commodity market are all good heartland, conservative agricultural measures undertaken as risk prevention, not as flyers in a volatile market. However, what was an ordered, conservative approach to hedging in the 1800s began developing rapidly and spectacularly in some areas as wild speculation in the late 1900s. During 1994, some investors and registrants experienced significant, and sometimes unexpected, losses in market risk sensitive instruments due to, among other things, changes in interest rates, foreign currency exchange rates, and commodity prices. In light of these losses and the substantial growth in the use of market risk sensitive instruments, public disclosure about these instruments has emerged as an important issue in financial markets.

As mentioned, a portion of the SEC study on derivatives during 1994 and 1995 was a review of annual reports filed by approximately 500 registrants. The avowed purpose was to assess the quality of disclosures relating to market risk sensitive instruments and to determine what, if any, additional information was needed to improve disclosures about derivatives. They determined that partly because of FASB 119, disclosures reviewed in 1995 were more informative than those reviewed in 1994.

THREE BASIC PROPOSALS

It was the opinion of those reviewing the situation that the three aforementioned significant disclosure issues remain as problems. To address these specific disclosure issues, the SEC has proposed guidance reminders and amendments to their basic regulations:

1) Amendments to Regulation S-X requiring enhanced descriptions in the footnotes to the financial statements of accounting policies for derivative financial instruments and derivative commodity instruments. These disclosures would be required unless the registrant's derivative activities are not material. The materiality of derivatives activities would be measured by the fair values of derivative financial instruments and derivative commodity instruments at the end of each reporting period and the fair value of those instruments during each reporting period.

2) Amendments creating a new item within Regulation S-K requiring disclosure outside the financial statements of qualitative and quantitative information about derivative financial instruments, other financial instruments, and derivative commodity instruments. These disclosures would be required if the fair values of market risk sensitive instruments outstanding at the end of the current reporting period were material or the potential loss in future earnings, fair values, or cash flows of market risk sensitive instruments from reasonably possible market movements appeared likely to be material.

3) Reminders to registrants that when they provide disclosure about financial instruments, commodity positions, firm commitments, and other

anticipated transactions, *reported items*, such disclosure must include information about derivatives that affect directly or indirectly such reported items, to the extent the effects of such information is material and necessary to prevent the disclosure about the reported item from being misleading. For example, when information is required to be disclosed in the footnotes to the financial statements about interest rates and repricing characteristics of debt obligations, registrants should include, when material, disclosure of the effects of derivatives. Similarly, summary information and disclosures in MD&A about the cost of debt obligations should include, when material, disclosure of the effects of derivatives.

SAFE HARBOR PROVISIONS

Concern has been expressed in several quarters that disclosing information about market risk may have legal ramifications for registrants if actual outcomes differ from the market risk amounts disclosed. The Commission indicated its intention that forward-looking disclosures made pursuant to the proposed new requirement of Regulation S-K and and the related item of Form 20-F be subject to an appropriate safe harbor. Congress recently adopted the Private Securities Litigation Reform Act of 1995. (Discussed in Chapter 11.) Among other things, it amends the Securities Act and Securities Exchange Act to include a safe harbor for *forward-looking information.* The SEC is continuing to consider how best to draft an appropriate safe harbor in line with this recent legislation, and indicated it intends to add to their proposals a provision that the disclosures, if required by new rules, be made subject to safe harbor provisions.

SMALL BUSINESS ISSUERS

The Commission believes that because of the newness and evolving nature of these disclosures, as well as the relative costs of complying with them, that it is appropriate, at this time, to exempt small business issuers from the proposed disclosures of quantitative and qualitative information about market risk. Accordingly, at this time, the Commission is *not* proposing to amend Regulation S-B to incorporate an item similar to the proposed new item of Regulation S-K. Small business issuers, however, still would be required to comply with the following:

1) The proposed amendment regarding accounting policies disclosures for derivatives.

2) The suggested proposal that registrants provide additional information about the effects of derivatives on information expressly required to be filed with the Commission.

3) To the extent market risk represents a known trend, event, or uncertainty, to discuss the impact of market risk on past and future financial condition and results of operations, pursuant to Item 303 of Regulation S-B.

LACK OF DIRECTION NOTED

The SEC study revealed that in the absence of comprehensive requirements for accounting for derivatives, registrants are developing accounting practices for options and complex derivatives by piecemeal application of the various APB Opinions, FASB Statements, EITF Issues, and the limited amount of such literature that does exist.

The varied applications are complicated because existing derivative literature refers to at least three distinctly different methods of accounting for derivatives: fair value accounting, deferral accounting, and accrual accounting. Further, the underlying concepts and criteria used in determining the applicability of these accounting methods are not consistent.

To illustrate: Under the fair value method, derivatives are carried on the balance sheet at fair value with changes in that value recognized in earnings or stockholders' equity; see, e.g., FASB 52, *Foreign Currency Translation*, and FASB 80, *Accounting for Futures Contracts*. Under the deferral method, gains and losses from derivatives are deferred on the balance sheet and recognized in earnings in conjunction with earnings of designated items, FASB 52 and FASB 80. Under the accrual method, each net payment or receipt due or owed under the derivative is recognized in earnings during the period to which the payment or receipt relates; there is no recognition on the balance sheet for changes in the derivative's fair value.

Things get even more convoluted—the risk reduction criterion in FASB 52 is different from the risk reduction criterion in FASB 80. FASB 52 specifies risk reduction on a transaction basis while FASB 80 specifies risk reduction on an enterprise basis. In addition, FASB 80 permits the use of deferral accounting for futures contracts used to hedge probable, but not firmly committed, anticipated transactions, while FASB 52 prohibits deferral accounting for foreign currency forward exchange contracts used to hedge those same types of anticipated transactions. (Also, see the discussion of FASB Statements 52 and 80 in *ADB*, Chapter 10.)

As a result of lack of consistent direction during its 1994–1995 reviews of filings, the SEC staff observed that registrants, in attempting to interpret the literature, were accounting for the same type of derivative in many different ways.

(We assume that it remained a moot question as to whether the interpretation was based on evidence of advantage to the registrant.) Thus, it was difficult to compare the financial statement effects of derivatives across registrants.

BUILDING ON FASB 119

In order to provide a better understanding of the accounting for derivative financial instruments, FASB 119 requires disclosure of the policies used to account for such instruments, in line with the requirements of APB 22. Specifically, FASB 119 emphasizes the disclosure of policies for recognizing, or not recognizing, and measuring derivative financial instruments. When recognized, the location of where those instruments and related gains and losses are reported in the statements of financial position and income must be clearly indicated.

However, FASB 119 does not provide explicit instruction concerning what must be disclosed in accounting policies footnotes to make more understandable the effects of derivatives on the statements of financial position, cash flows, and results of operations; and it does not address disclosure of accounting policies for derivative commodity instruments. Thus, to facilitate a more informed assessment of the effects of derivatives on financial statements, the proposed amendments make explicit the items to be disclosed in the accounting policies footnotes for derivative financial instruments and derivative commodity instruments.

PROPOSED DISCLOSURE RULE IN REGULATION S-X

The Commission proposes amendments to Regulation S-X requiring enhanced descriptions in the footnotes to the financial statements of accounting policies for derivative financial instruments and derivative commodity instruments. These disclosures would be required unless the registrant's derivative activities are not material. For this proposal, the materiality of derivatives activities would be measured by the fair values of derivative financial instruments and derivative commodity instruments at the end of each reporting period and the fair value of those instruments during each reporting period.

The proposed amendments pertaining to accounting policies would add a new paragraph to Regulation S-X to require disclosure in the footnotes to the financial statements relating:

1) Each method used to account for derivatives.
2) Types of derivatives accounted for under each method.
3) The criteria required to be met for each accounting method used (e.g., the manner in which risk reduction, correlation, designation, and/or effectiveness tests are applied).

4) The accounting method used if the specified criteria are not met.

5) The accounting for the termination of derivatives designated as hedges or used to affect directly or indirectly the terms, fair values, or cash flows of a designated item.

6) The accounting for derivatives if the designated item matures, or is sold, extinguished, terminated, or, if related to an anticipated transaction, is no longer likely to occur.

7) Where and when derivatives and their related gains and losses are reported in the statements of financial position, cash flows, and results of operations.

The proposed amendments would require registrants to distinguish between accounting policies used for derivatives entered into for trading purposes, and those that are entered into for purposes other than trading.

Disclosure of accounting policies for derivatives would be required unless the registrant's derivative activities are not material. For this proposal, the materiality of derivatives activities would be measured by the fair values of derivative financial instruments and derivative commodity instruments at the end of each reporting period and the fair value of those instruments during each reporting period. In essence, the proposed amendments clarify the application of the accounting policy disclosure requirements set forth in FASB 119 for derivative financial instruments. They also extend those requirements to the disclosure of accounting policies for derivative commodity instruments.

DISCLOSURE OF QUANTITATIVE AND QUALITATIVE INFORMATION ABOUT MARKET RISK IN REGULATION S-K

The Commission proposes amendments creating a new item in Regulation S-K requiring disclosure outside the financial statements of *quantitative* and *qualitative* information about derivative financial instruments, other financial instruments, and derivative commodity instruments. If any of the following items are material, these disclosures would be required:

1) The fair values of market risk sensitive instruments outstanding at the end of the current reporting period.

2) The potential loss in future earnings, fair values, or cash flows of market risk sensitive instruments from reasonably possible market movements.

In complying with the proposed amendments requiring disclosure of *quantitative* information about market risk, registrants would be permitted to select any one of the following three disclosure alternatives:

1) Tabular presentation of expected future cash flow amounts and related contract terms categorized by expected maturity dates.

2) Sensitivity analysis expressing the possible loss in earnings, fair values, or cash flows of market risk sensitive instruments from selected hypothetical changes in market rates and prices.

3) Value at risk disclosures expressing the potential loss in earnings, fair values, or cash flows of market risk sensitive instruments from market movements over a selected period of time with a selected likelihood of occurrence.

The proposed *qualitative* information about market risk would include a narrative discussion of:

1) A registrant's primary market risk exposures.

2) How the registrant manages those exposures; e.g., a description of the objectives, general strategies, and instruments, if any, used to manage those exposures.

3) Changes in either the registrant's primary market risk exposures or how those exposures are managed when compared to what was in effect during the most recent reporting period and what is known or expected to be in effect in future reporting periods.

Market risk is inherent in *both derivative and nonderivative* instruments, including:

1) Other financial instruments, comprised of nonderivative financial instruments such as investments, loans, structured notes, mortgage-backed securities, indexed instruments, interest-only and principal-only obligations, deposits, and other debt obligations.

2) Derivative financial instruments—futures, forwards, swaps, options, and other financial instruments with similar characteristics.

3) Derivative commodity instruments that are reasonably possible to be settled in cash or with another financial instrument including commodity futures, commodity forwards, commodity swaps, commodity options, and other commodity instruments with similar characteristics, to the extent such instruments are not derivative financial instruments.

Generally accepted accounting principles (GAAP) and SEC rules require disclosure of certain *quantitative* information about some of these derivative financial instruments. For example, registrants are currently required to disclose notional amounts of derivative financial instruments and the nature and terms of debt obligations. However, this information is often abbreviated, is presented piecemeal in different parts of the financial statements, and does not apply to all market risk sensitive instruments. Thus, investors often are unable to determine whether, if, or how particular financial and commodity instruments actually affect a registrant's net market risk exposure. FASB 119 encourages, but does not require, disclosure of quantitative information about the overall market risk inherent in derivative financial instruments and other instruments subject to market risk. Therefore, implementation of this portion of the proposed amendments is spelled out in detail for both quantitative and qualitative disclosure.

QUANTITATIVE DISCLOSURE

To allow investors to assess overall market risk more easily, the proposed amendments would create a new SEC requirement for disclosure, *outside* the financial statements, of *quantitative* market risk information for derivative financial instruments, other financial instruments, and derivative commodity instruments. As indicated above, this information would be furnished using one of the following three ways, at the election of the registrant:

TABULAR PRESENTATION

This first quantitative market risk disclosure alternative would permit registrants to provide a tabular presentation of terms and information related to derivative financial instruments, other financial instruments, and derivative commodity instruments. Such information would include, but would not be limited to, fair values of instruments, expected principal or transaction cash flows, weighted average effective rates or prices, and other relevant market risk related information. These data are common inputs to market risk measurement methods and, therefore, may be useful in understanding a registrant's exposure to market risk. This tabular information would be summarized by risk exposure category; i.e., interest rate risk, foreign currency exchange rate risk, commodity price risk, and other similar price risks, such as equity price risk, and, within the foreign currency exchange rate risk category, by functional currency; e.g., U.S. dollar or Japanese yen. FASB 119 lists five possible quantitative methods of measuring and disclosing market risk, but the SEC study discovered that, in fact, many companies are *not* making these disclosures. Recommended methods include:

1) Details about current positions and perhaps activity during the period.
2) The hypothetical effects on equity, or on annual income, of several possible changes in market price.
3) A gap analysis of interest rate repricing or maturity dates.
4) The duration of the financial instruments.

5) The entity's value at risk from derivative financial instruments and from other positions at the end of the reporting period and the average value at risk during the year.

In each of these risk exposure categories, instruments should be grouped based on common characteristics. At a minimum, instruments should be distinguished by the following characteristics:

1) Fixed rate or variable rate assets or liabilities.
2) Long or short forwards or futures.
3) Written or purchased put or call options.
4) Receive fixed or receive variable interest rate swaps.
5) The currency in which the instruments' cash flows are denominated.

Thus, for example, within the interest rate risk exposure category, a company might present the following list of instruments: fixed rate Mexican peso investments, variable rate U.S. dollar debt obligations, long U.S. Treasury futures, and Mexican peso receive variable interest rate swaps.

For each instrument included in the tabulation, expected principal or transaction cash flow information would be presented separately for each of the next five years, with the remaining expected cash flows presented as an aggregate amount. The proposed amendments also would require disclosure of information on assumptions necessary to an understanding of a registrant's tabular market risk disclosures. In this regard, registrants would describe, at a minimum, the differing numbers reported in the table for various categories of instruments; e.g., principal cash flows for debt, notional amounts for swaps, contract amounts for options and futures, and key prepayment and/or reinvestment assumptions relating to the timing of reported cash flow amounts.

Derivatives used to manage risks inherent in anticipated transactions also should be disclosed separately, with a description of assumptions necessary to understand the disclosures.

At the current time, the Commission is not proposing to prescribe standardized methods and procedures specifying how to comply with each of these disclosure alternatives. To the extent registrants use one of these methods internally, they would be permitted, but not required, to report quantitative measures of market risk using the same method externally. To facilitate comparisons between companies, the Commission proposes that they provide descriptions of the model and assumptions used to prepare quantitative market risk disclosures.

SENSITIVITY ANALYSIS

The second quantitative market risk disclosure alternative would permit companies to provide disclosure of sensitivity analysis that expresses the hypothetical loss in future earnings, fair values, or cash flows of market risk sensitive instruments over the next reporting period due to hypothetical changes in interest rates, currency exchange rates, commodity prices, and other similar market price changes; e.g., equity prices. These disclosures may be similar to the interest rate *sensitivity* measures already required for regulatory purposes for thrift institutions. Under the proposed amendments, earnings, fair values, or cash flows, sensitivity disclosures would be presented separately for interest rate sensitive instruments, currency exchange rate sensitive instruments, certain commodity price sensitive instruments, and other types of market risk sensitive instruments like equity instruments.

The proposed amendments also would require disclosure of the assumptions and parameters underlying the registrant's sensitivity analysis model that are needed to understand the company's market risk disclosure. At a minimum, the following information should be provided:

1) How loss is defined by the model—loss in earnings, fair values, cash flows.

2) A general description of the modeling technique—change in net present values arising from parallel shifts in market rates or prices, how optionality is addressed by the model.

3) The general types of instruments covered by the model—derivative financial instruments, other financial instruments, derivative commodity instruments—and whether other instruments are included voluntarily in the model by the registrant, such as certain commodity instruments and positions, cash flows from anticipated transactions, and operating cash, flows from nonfinancial, noncommodity instruments.

4) Other relevant information on model parameters—possibly, the magnitudes of parallel shifts in market rates or prices used for each category of market risk exposure, the method by which discount rates are determined, and key prepayment and/or reinvestment assumptions.

In summary, the magnitude of each selected hypothetical change in rates or prices may differ across risk exposures. Separate sensitivity analysis disclosures should be made for each category of risk exposure. A description of the model assumptions and parameters necessary to an understanding of the resulting disclosures should be included.

VALUE AT RISK

The third quantitative disclosure alternative would permit registrants to provide value at risk disclosures expressing the potential entity-wide loss in fair values, earnings, or cash flows of market risk sensitive instruments that might arise from adverse market movements with a selected likelihood of occurrence over a selected time interval.

Additional separate value at risk disclosures would be required for interest rate sensitive instruments, currency exchange rate sensitive instruments, certain commodity price sensitive instruments, and other similar market risk sensitive instruments; e.g., equities. In addition, to help place reported value at risk amounts in context, registrants would be required to report either:

1) The average or range in the value at risk numbers for the reported period.
2) The average or range in actual changes in fair values, earnings, or cash flows of instruments occurring during the reporting period.
3) The percentage of time the actual changes in fair values, earnings, or cash flows of market risk sensitive instruments exceeded the reported value at risk amounts during the current reporting period.

This information would not be required for the first fiscal year-end if or when the rule is put into effect. A description of the model assumptions and parameters necessary to an understanding of these disclosures should also be included.

The proposed amendments also would require disclosure of the model assumptions and parameters underlying the registrant's value at risk model that are necessary to an understanding of the registrant's market risk disclosure. In this regard, registrants would specify, at a minimum:

1) How loss is defined by the model; e.g., loss in fair values, earnings, or cash flows.
2) A general description of the modeling technique; e.g., variance or covariance, historical simulation, Monte Carlo simulation, and how optionality is addressed by the model.
3) The general types of instruments covered by the model; e.g., derivative financial instruments, other financial instruments, derivative commodity instruments, and whether other instruments are included voluntarily in the model by the registrant, such as certain commodity instruments and positions, cash flows from anticipated transactions, and operating cash flows from nonfinancial and noncommodity instruments.
4) Other material information on model parameters; e.g., holding period, confidence interval, and the method used for aggregating value at risk amounts across market risk exposure categories, such as by assuming perfect positive correlation, independence, or by using actual observed correlations.

DIFFERENTIATION BETWEEN SENSITIVITY ANALYSIS AND VALUE AT RISK

The SEC study points out that the primary difference between the value at risk and sensitivity methods are that the former reports the potential loss arising from equally likely market movements across instruments, while sensitivity analysis reports the likelihood of occurrence across instruments; and value at risk explicitly adjusts the potential loss to reflect correlations between market movements, while sensitivity analysis is not designed explicitly to make such adjustments.

General Considerations on Quantitative Disclosure

In addition to selecting and utilizing one of the alternative quantitative market risk disclosure methods discussed above, registrants would be required to discuss material limitations that could cause that information not to reflect the overall market risk of the entity. This discussion would necessarily include descriptions of each limitation, and, if applicable, the instruments' features that are not reflected fully within the selected quantitative market risk disclosure alternative.

Registrants would also be required to summarize information for the preceding fiscal year, and discuss the reasons for any material changes in quantitative information about market risk when compared to the information reported in the previous period. Provision is made for companies to change their method of presentation of the quantitative information from one to another of the three alternatives. However, if they do change, they must explain why they changed, and summarize comparable information under the new method for the year preceding the year of the change.

Qualitative Information About Market Risk

A *qualitative* discussion of a registrant's market risk exposures and how those exposures are managed is important to an understanding of a registrant's market risk. Such qualitative disclosures help place market risk management activities in the context of the business and, therefore, are a useful complement to quantitative information about market risk. FASB 119 requires that certain qualitative disclosures be provided about market risk management activities associated with derivative financial instruments held or issued for purposes other than trading. In particular, it requires disclosure of the entity's objectives for holding or issuing the derivative financial instruments, the context needed to understand those objectives, and its general strategies for achieving those objectives. In addition, Statement 119 requires separate disclosures about derivative financial instruments used as hedges of anticipated transactions. As indicated above, these requirements apply only to certain derivatives held or issued for purposes other than trading.

In essence, the proposed qualitative disclosure requirements would create a new requirement in Regulation S-K, which would expand certain FASB 119 disclosures to:

1) Encompass derivative commodity instruments, other financial instruments, and derivative financial instruments entered into for trading purposes.

2) Require registrants to evaluate and describe material changes in their primary risk exposures and material changes in how those exposures are managed.

In particular, the proposed amendments would require narrative disclosure outside the financial statements of:

1) A registrant's primary market risk exposures.

2) How those exposures are managed; e.g., a description of the objectives, general strategies, and instruments, if any, used to manage those exposures.

In preparing the proposed qualitative disclosures about market risk, the Commission expects registrants to describe their primary market risk exposures as they exist at the end of the current reporting period and how those risks are currently being managed. Registrants also would be required to describe material changes in their primary market risk exposures and material changes in how these risks are managed as compared to what was in effect during the most recent reporting period and what is known or expected to be in effect in future reporting periods.

These proposed qualitative disclosure requirements would apply to derivative financial instruments, other financial instruments, and derivative commodity instruments. As in the case with respect to the quantitative disclosures about market risk, the qualitative disclosures should be presented separately for market risk sensitive instruments that are entered into for trading purposes and those that are entered into for purposes other than trading. In addition, qualitative information about market risk should be presented separately for those instruments used to manage risks inherent in anticipated transactions.

Finally, to help make disclosures about market risk more comprehensive, as is the case with the quantitative disclosures, the Commission also is proposing to encourage registrants to disclose qualitative information about market risk relating to other items, such as derivative commodity instruments not reasonably possible to be settled in cash or with another financial instrument, commodity positions, cash flows from anticipated transactions, and operating cash flows from nonfinancial and noncommodity instruments; e.g., cash flows generated by manufacturing activities.

GENERAL ACCOUNTING OFFICE (GAO): FINANCIAL DERIVATIVES

Appearing before various Congressional committees in 1994, top ranking officials of the U.S. General Accounting Office pointed out that in the past two decades, fundamental changes in global financial markets—particularly the increased volatility of interest rates and currency exchange rates—prompted a number of public and private institutions to develop and use derivatives. Further, derivatives use has been expanding rapidly as a result of continuing globalization of commerce and financial markets and major advances in finance, information processing, and communications technology.

What Are Derivatives?

Derivatives are financial products whose values are based on the value of an underlying asset, reference rate, or index. The GAO focused on the four basic types of derivatives from which the more exotic ones have been developed: forwards, futures, options, and swaps. Some derivatives are standardized contracts traded on exchanges. Others are customized contracts that include negotiated terms, such as amounts, payment timing, and interest or currency rates. Those contracts that are not traded on an exchange, are classified as over-the-counter (OTC) derivatives.

Function of Derivatives

Even those who are most concerned about the problems that derivatives can present agree that they serve important functions in the global financial marketplace. They are not about to go away; therefore, the only "solution" is to understand better their nature, attributes, dangers, and weakness. Basically, derivatives offer two benefits:

1) They provide the time-honored process of hedging to the end-user to manage financial risk better.
2) They offer the opportunity to speculate on market prices or rates.

Among their benefits, derivatives provide end-users with opportunities to better manage financial risks associated with business transactions such as hedging. They also provide opportunities to profit from anticipated movements in market prices or rates through judicious speculating.

Derivative activities have grown into sums in the trillions in notional amounts—however misleading notional values may be. This unquestioned growth and the increasing complexity of derivatives reflect both the increased demand from end-users for better ways to manage their financial risks and the innovative capacity of the financial services industry to respond to market demands.

Derivatives' Risks

Because of the phenomenal and sometimes disastrous derivatives growth and complexity, Congress, federal regulators, and some members of the industry have become increasingly concerned about the risks derivatives pose to the financial system, individual firms, investors, and U.S. taxpayers. These concerns were heightened by the reports of substantial losses by some derivatives end-users, including losses totaling in the hundreds of millions of dollars by U.S. firms, both large and small.

In their study, the GAO had decided that much OTC derivatives activity in the United States was concentrated among 15 major U.S. dealers that are extensively linked to one another, end-users, and the exchange-traded markets. For example, they found that the top seven domestic bank OTC derivatives dealers accounted for more than 90 percent of total U.S. bank derivatives activity. Similarly, securities regulatory data indicated that the top five U.S. securities firms dealing in OTC derivatives accounted for about 87 percent of total derivatives activity for all U.S. securities firms.

Substantial linkages also existed between these major U.S. derivatives dealers and foreign derivatives dealers. The GAO received information from 14 major U.S. OTC derivatives dealers that transactions with foreign dealers represented an average of about 24 percent of their combined derivatives notional amounts.

This combination of global involvement, concentration, and linkages suggested that the sudden failure or abrupt withdrawal from trading of any of those large U.S. dealers could cause liquidity problems in the markets and could also pose risks to the others, including federally insured banks and the financial system as a whole. Although the federal government would not necessarily intervene just to keep a major OTC derivatives dealer from failing, the federal government would be likely to intervene to keep the financial system functioning in cases of severe financial stress. While federal regulators have often been able to keep financial disruptions from becoming crises, in some cases intervention has necessitated and could again result in a financial bailout paid for or guaranteed by taxpayers.

GAO Concerns

The GAO report emphasized that primary responsibility for effective management of a firm's financial risks rests within the firm itself—with boards of directors and senior management. A system of strong corporate governance, such as that required under the FDIC Improvement Act for large banks and thrifts, is particularly critical for managing derivatives activities, because they can affect the financial well-being of the entire firm. Until recently, however, there were no comprehensive guidelines against which boards and senior managers could measure their firm's risk management performance. In 1993, a Group of Thirty-sponsored study identified improvements that were needed in derivatives risk management and recommended benchmark practices for the industry. The Office of the Comptroller of the

Currency and the Federal Reserve also issued guidelines for the banks they oversee.

Regulators and market participants felt that improvements in risk management systems had already been made as a result of the Group of Thirty recommendations and federal guidelines. However, the GAO pointed out that no regulatory mechanism existed to bring all major dealers into compliance with these recommendations and guidelines. Further, the Office felt that while actions which the major dealers reported taking were commendable and important, the federal government also has responsibility for ensuring that safeguards exist to require compliance with certain standards to protect the overall financial system.

Federal regulators have begun to address derivatives activities through a variety of means, but significant gaps and weaknesses exist in the regulation of many major dealers. The GAO has been concerned that securities regulators have limited authority to regulate the financial activities of securities firm affiliates that conduct OTC derivatives activities. Insurance companies' OTC derivatives affiliates are subject to limited state regulation and have no federal oversight. Yet these relatively "unregulated" OTC derivatives affiliates of securities and insurance firms constitute a rapidly growing component of the derivatives markets.

In contrast to insurance and securities regulators, bank regulators have authority to supervise all the financial activities of banks and their holding companies. While these regulators have improved their supervision of banks' derivatives activities, their approach still has weaknesses, such as inadequate regulatory reporting requirements and insufficient documentation and testing of internal controls and systems.

Are Accounting Standards Inadequate?

The GAO became particularly concerned about the lack of adequate accounting standards and financial reporting requirements. They felt that this further compounded the regulators' problems and contributed to the lack of knowledge by investors, creditors, and other market participants specifically because of the inadequate rules for financial reporting of derivatives activity. They found that accounting standards for derivatives, particularly those used for hedging purposes by end users, were incomplete and inconsistent and not keeping pace with business practices. They also found that additional disclosures were needed to provide a clear distinction between dealing, speculative, and hedging activities, and to quantify interest rate and other market risks. The report made it clear that the GAO considers that insufficient accounting rules and disclosure for derivatives increase the likelihood that financial reports will not fairly represent the substance and risk potential of these complex activities. In addition, the lack of rules for certain types of derivatives makes it likely that accounting for these products will be inconsistent, thereby greatly reducing the comparability of financial reports.

At the time of this report, the comment deadline was approaching for FASB 119, *Disclosure About Derivative Financial Instruments and Fair Value of Financial Instruments*. The GAO report commented that, although it was an improvement over existing disclosure requirements in FASB 105, *Disclosure of Information About Financial Instruments with Off-Balance-Sheet Risk and Financial Instruments with Concentrations of Credit Risk, and FASB 107, Disclosure About Fair Value of Financial Instruments*, it was not enough. Deficiencies cited by the GAO report of what was to become FASB 119 included:

1) A lack of a clear distinction between dealing activities, speculative activities, and hedging and other risk management activities necessary for a clear understanding of the nature and risks of companies' derivatives activities.

2) It encouraged, but did not require that the risks of interest rate and other market changes be quantified and disclosed. They felt those disclosures should be *required* because of the significant risk that such market changes pose to many companies.

3) Even though the disclosure picture was improving, consistent and comprehensive accounting rules that would require such risks to be reflected in the derivation of financial statement figures were lacking.

The GAO believes that innovation and creativity are strengths of the U.S. financial services industry and that these strengths should not be eroded or forced outside the United States by excessive regulation. However, they also believe the regulatory gaps and weaknesses that presently exist must be addressed, especially considering the rapid growth in derivatives activity. The issue is one of striking a proper balance between sometimes opposing forces by:

1) Allowing the U.S. financial services industry to grow and innovate.
2) Protecting the safety and soundness of the nation's financial system.

Achieving this balance will require unprecedented cooperation among U.S. and foreign regulators, market participants, and members of the accounting profession, according to the GAO.

Federal Regulation Is Needed

Given the lack of explicit direction that impedes regulatory preparedness for dealing with a financial crisis associated with derivatives, they recommended that Congress require federal regulation of the safety and soundness of all major U.S. OTC derivatives dealers. They considered that the immediate need is for Congress to bring the OTC derivatives activities of securities and insurance firm affiliates under the purview of one or more of the existing federal financial regulators and to ensure that derivatives regulation is consistent and comprehensive across regulatory agencies. They also recommended that the financial regulators take specific actions to improve their capabilities to oversee OTC activities and to anticipate or respond to any financial crisis involving derivatives. They emphasized that the major derivatives dealers and end users should be concerned about the need for improved accounting standards and disclosure requirements for derivatives activities.

While their recommendations addressed regulatory gaps and weaknesses in the context of the current regulatory system, the nature of derivatives activities demonstrates in their opinion that this system has not kept pace with the dramatic and rapid changes that are occurring in domestic and global financial markets. Banking, securities, futures, and insurance are no longer separate and distinct areas that can be well regulated by the existing patchwork quilt of federal and state agencies. Therefore, they also recommended to Congress that it should begin systematically to address the need to revamp and modernize the entire U.S. regulatory system.

Even though the GAO's recommendations to Congress and the federal financial regulators are beyond the purview of this Supplement, the recommendations to the FASB and the SEC at the time of this report do seem pertinent.

Recommendations to the FASB:

1) Proceed expeditiously to issue the existing exposure draft on disclosure of derivatives and fair value of financial instruments.

2) Proceed expeditiously to develop and issue an exposure draft that provides comprehensive, consistent accounting rules for derivative products, including expanded disclosure requirements that provide additional needed information about derivative activities.

3) Consider adopting a market value accounting model for all financial instruments, including derivative products.

Recommendations to the SEC:

1) Ensure that SEC registrants that are major end-users of complex derivative products establish and implement corporate requirements for independent, knowledgeable audit committees and public reporting on internal controls. Internal control reporting by boards of directors, managers, and external auditors should include assessments of derivatives risk management systems.

2) Ensure that the FASB proceeds expeditiously to develop and adopt comprehensive, consistent accounting rules and disclosure requirements for derivative products.

Chapter 3
IRAs, Pension, and Annuity Income

INDIVIDUAL RETIREMENT ARRANGEMENTS

This discussion includes an explanation of the IRS requirements that apply to IRAs. Also included are the regulations for reporting pension and annuity income on a federal income tax return, and the topic covers the special tax treatment of lump-sum distributions from pension, stock bonus, and profit-sharing plans, and for rollovers from qualified employer plans. An *individual retirement arrangement (IRA)* allows taxpayers advantages to save money for retirement by deducting contributions to an IRA in whole or in part, depending on the taxpayer's circumstances. The amounts set aside, including earnings and gains, are not taxed until distributed to the saver.

An individual can establish an IRA if he or she has taxable compensation during the year and has not reached age 70 $1/2$ by the end of the year. Compensation includes wages, salaries, tips, commissions, fees, bonuses, taxable alimony, and separate maintenance payments. One can also set up an IRA for one's spouse. The following types of IRAs can be used:

1) Individual Retirement Account. This plan is set up with any financial institution that meets the requirements of the Internal Revenue Code.
2) Individual Retirement Annuity. This plan is set up by purchasing a special annuity contract from a life insurance company.
3) Employer and Employee Association Trust Account. An employer, labor union, or other employee association can set up an individual retirement account for an individual.

4) Simplified Employee Pension (SEP). Under an SEP plan, an employer can establish an individual retirement account called an *SEP-IRA* for an employee that allows the employer to contribute to it each year and deduct up to 15% of the employee's compensation, or $30,000, whichever is less. A self-employed person is treated as an employee for this purpose.

INDIVIDUAL RETIREMENT ACCOUNT

An individual retirement account is a trust or custodial account set up in the United States for the *exclusive benefit* of the person setting it up, or for the benefit of the person's beneficiaries. The account is created by a written document, which must show how the account meets all of the following requirements:

1) The trustee or custodian must be a bank, a federally insured credit union, a savings and loan association, or an entity approved by the IRS to act as trustee or custodian.

2) The trustee or custodian generally cannot accept contributions of more than $2,000 a year. However, rollover contributions and employer contributions to a simplified employee pension (SEP) can be more than $2,000. An SEP is a written arrangement that allows an employee's employer to make a deductible contribution to an IRA, which is identified as an SEP-IRA.

3) The holder's contributions must be in cash, except that rollover contributions can be property other than cash.

4) The amount in the account must be fully vested and the holder must have a nonforfeitable right to the amount at all times.

5) Money in the account cannot be used to buy a life insurance policy.

6) Assets in the account cannot be combined with other property, except in a common trust fund or common investment fund.

7) The holder must start receiving distributions from his or her account by April 1 of the year following the year in which the holder becomes 70 $\frac{1}{2}$.

INDIVIDUAL RETIREMENT ANNUITY

An individual retirement annuity can be set up by purchasing an annuity contract or an endowment contract from a life insurance company. The annuity must be issued in the holder's name as the owner, and either the holder or surviving beneficiaries are the only ones who can receive the benefits or payments. An individual retirement annuity must meet the following requirements:

1) The holder's entire interest in the contract must be nonforfeitable.

2) It must provide that no portion of the annuity can be transferred to any person other than the issuer.

3) It must have flexible premiums so that if the holder's compensation changes, payments can also change.

4) It must provide that the holder cannot contribute more than $2,000 in any year. Premium refunds are used to pay for future premiums, or to buy more benefits before the end of the calendar year after the year the refund was paid.

5) It must *begin* distribution by April of the year following the year in which the holder reaches age 70 $1/2$.

Employer and Employee Association Trust Accounts

An employer, labor union, or other employee association can set up a trust to provide individual retirement accounts for its employees or members. The rules for individual retirement accounts apply to these employer or union established IRAs.

Required Disclosures

The trustee or issuer, sometimes called the sponsor, of the IRA the holder chooses must give the holder a disclosure statement about the arrangement at least seven days before the IRA is set up. The sponsor can give the holder a statement by the date the IRA is set up if the holder is given at least seven days from that date to revoke the IRA. If the IRA is revoked within the revocation period, the sponsor must return the entire amount paid to the holder. The sponsor must report both the holder's contribution to the IRA and the distribution to the holder upon his or her revocation of the IRA.

How Much Can Be Contributed to an IRA?

An amount up to $2000, or 100% of a taxpayer's taxable income, whichever is less, can be contributed to an IRA each year. Whether contributions are deductible or nondeductible, the taxpayer must have received taxable compensation to make contributions to an IRA. The amount of a deduction depends on whether or not a taxpayer, or spouse, is covered by a retirement plan at work. If the taxpayer is covered, or considered covered, the deduction amount depends on his or her filing status and how much income he or she has. The taxpayer's income determines whether the taxpayer can take a full deduction, a partial deduction, or no deduction. (A table is available from the IRS district office in the taxpayer's area which lists the deduction limits for taxpayers who are single, head of household, married filing jointly, or married filing separately).

DEDUCTIBLE CONTRIBUTIONS

A taxpayer can take a deduction for an IRA contribution before actually making the contribution, but it must be made by the due date of the taxpayer's return, not including extensions. If the holder, or the holder's spouse, is covered by an employer loan at any time during the year, the allowable IRA deduction will be less than the allowable contributions. The allowable deduction can be reduced or eliminated, depending on the amount of the holder's income and his or her filing status.

EMPLOYER PLANS

An employer plan is one that an employer sets up for the benefit of the employees. For purposes of the IRA deduction rules, an employer retirement plan is any of the following:

1) A qualified pension, profit-sharing, stock bonus, money purchase pension plan, including Keogh plans. A qualified plan is one that meets Internal Revenue Code requirements.

2) A 401(k) plan which is an arrangement included in a profit-sharing or stock bonus plan that allows a holder to choose to take part of his or her compensation from the employer in cash or have the employer pay it into the plan.

3) A union plan, a qualified stock bonus, pension, or profit-sharing plan created by a collective bargaining arrangement between employee representatives and one or more employers.

4) A qualified annuity plan.

5) A plan established for its employees by the United States, a state or political subdivision thereof, or by an agency or instrumentality of any of the foregoing.

6) A tax-sheltered annuity plan for employees of public schools and certain tax-exempt organizations—a 403b plan.

7) A simplified employee pension (SEP) plan.

DEFINED BENEFIT PLAN

A defined benefit plan is any plan that is not a defined contribution plan. Contributions to a defined benefit plan are based on a computation of what contributions are necessary to provide definite benefits to plan participants. Defined benefit plans include pension plans and annuity plans. If an employee meets minimum age and years of service requirements to participate in the employer's defined benefit plan for the plan year that ends within the holder's tax year, then the holder is considered covered by the plan. This procedure applies even if the holder of the plan did not make a required contribution, or did not perform the minimum service required to accrue a benefit for the year.

DEFINED CONTRIBUTION PLAN

A contribution plan is one in which amounts are contributed or allocated to an account for the plan year that ends within the taxpayer's tax year. A contribution plan provides for a separate account for each person covered by the plan, and benefits are based only on amounts contributed to, or allocated to, each account. Types of defined contribution plans include profit-sharing plans and stock bonus plans.

MARITAL STATUS

A spouse of the holder of an employer retirement plan is considered covered by a plan. To determine whether a holder is covered by an employer retirement plan, the holder's spouse must wait until the last day of the year because a holder's filing status for the year depends on his or her marital status on the last day of the tax year.

WHEN IS AN EMPLOYEE NOT COVERED?

If neither an employee nor an employee's spouse is covered by an employer plan for any part of the year, the employee is not covered for this purpose in the following situations:

1) If an employee is married filing a separate return. The employee is not covered by an employer retirement plan even if the employee's spouse is covered by a plan.
2) Coverage under Social Security or Railroad Retirement does not count as coverage under an employer retirement plan in figuring the IRA deduction.

3) If an employee receives retirement benefits from a previous employer's plan, and that employee is not covered under another employer's plan, the employee is considered not covered by a plan.

ROLLOVERS

A rollover is a tax-free distribution to a holder of cash or other assets from one retirement program to another program. The amount rolled over tax-free, however, is taxable later when the new program pays the rollover amount to the holder or beneficiary. There are two kinds of rollover contributions to an IRA. In one, amounts received from one IRA are put into another IRA. In the other type, amounts received from an employer's qualified retirement plan can be rolled over into another employer's plan.

The rollover contribution must be made by the 60th day after the day the holder receives the distribution from his or her IRA, or an employer's plan. Amounts not rolled over within the 60-day period do not qualify for tax-free rollover retirement and must be treated as a taxable distribution from either the holder's IRA or an employer's plan. The amount not rolled over is taxable in the year distributed, not in the year the 60-day period expires. There is a 10% tax on premature distributions and a 15% tax on excess distributions.

A distribution can be taken from an IRA for a rollover contribution to another IRA *once* in any one-year period. The one-year period begins on the date the IRA distribution is received, not on the date the distribution is rolled over into another IRA. If the holder receives a rollover distribution from his or her employer's qualified profit-sharing, stock bonus plan, annuity plan, or tax-sheltered annuity plan, all or part of it can be rolled over into an IRA.

WITHDRAWAL—AGE 59 $^1/_2$ RULE

Assets—money or other property—can be withdrawn from an IRA after the holder reaches age 59 $^1/_2$ and before age 70 $^1/_2$ without penalty. If more than $150,000 is withdrawn in any one year, a 15% tax has to be paid on the amount that exceeds $150,000. However, assets do not have to be withdrawn before age 70 $^1/_2$.

The *exceptions* to the age 59 $^1/_2$ rule for distributions are designed to provide relief from hardship situations such as disability and death. There is also an exception for distributions that are a part of a series of substantially equal payments. If the holder becomes disabled before reaching age 59 $^1/_2$, any amount can be withdrawn from an IRA without being subject to the 10% tax penalty. The holder must furnish proof that he or she cannot do any substantial gainful activity because of a physical or mental condition. A physician must determine that the holder's condition can be expected to result in death or to be of long continued and indefinite duration. If a holder's death occurs before reaching age 59 $\frac{1}{2}$, the assets in his or her IRA can be distributed to the beneficiary or to the holder's estate without having to pay the 10% additional tax. If the spouse inherits an IRA from a deceased holder, any distribution received before age 59 $\frac{1}{2}$ is subject to the 10% additional tax.

PROHIBITED TRANSACTIONS

A prohibited transaction is any improper use of an individual retirement account or annuity by the holder of the IRA or by any disqualified person. Examples of disqualified persons are:

1) The holder's fiduciary.
2) Members of the holder's family.

Examples of prohibited transactions with an IRA are:

1) Borrowing money from it.
2) Selling property to it.
3) Receiving unreasonable compensation for managing it.
4) Using it as security for a loan.
5) Buying property for personal use with IRA funds.

PENSION AND ANNUITY INCOME

This discussion explains how to report pension and annuity income on a federal income tax return, and covers the special tax treatment of lump-sum distributions from pension, stock bonus, and profit-sharing plans, and rollovers from *qualified* employer plans.

SOME DEFINITIONS

A *pension* is a series of payments made to an employee after he or she has retired from work. Pension payments are made regularly and are for past services with the employer.

An *annuity* is a series of payments under a contract. An employee can buy the contract alone, or can buy it with the help of his or her employer. Annuity payments are made regularly for more than one full year.

A *qualified employee plan* is an employer's stock bonus, pension, or profit-sharing plan that is for the exclusive benefit of employees or their beneficiaries. This plan must meet Internal Revenue Code requirements. It qualifies for special tax benefits, including tax deferral for employer contributions and rollover distributions, and capital gain treatment of the 5- or 10-year tax option for lump-sum distributions.

A *qualified employee annuity plan* is a retirement annuity purchased by an employee under a plan that meets Internal Revenue Code requirements.

A *tax-sheltered annuity plan* is a special annuity contract purchased for an employee of a public school or tax-exempt organization.

A *nonqualified employee plan* is an employer's plan that does not meet Internal Revenue Code requirements; it does not qualify for most of the tax benefits of a *qualified* plan.

Particular types of pensions and annuities include:

1) Fixed Person Annuities. The person receives definite amounts at regular intervals for a definite length of time.

2) Annuities for a Single Life. The annuitant receives definite amounts at regular intervals for life. The payments end at death.

3) Joint and Survivor Annuities. The first annuitant receives a definite amount at regular intervals for life. After he or she dies, a second annuitant receives a definite amount at regular intervals for life. The amount paid to the second annuitant may or may not differ from the amount paid to the first annuitant.

4) Variable Annuities. The annuitant receives payments that can vary in amount for a definite length of time or for life. The amount the annuitant receives depends upon such variables as profits earned by the pension or annuity funds, or cost-of-living indexes.

5) Disability Pensions. A person who is under the minimum retirement age can receive payments because the person is retired on disability.

SIMPLIFIED GENERAL RULE

The Simplified General Rule can be used by a retired employee or the survivor receiving a survivor annuity of an employee who died. In the case of a survivor of a deceased retiree, the Simplified General Rule can be used if the retiree used it. The simpler method can be used to figure the taxability of an annuity only if:

1) The annuity starting date is after July 1, 1986.

2) The annuity payments are for either the annuitant's life or the life of the annuitant's beneficiary.

3) The annuity payments are from a qualified employee plan, a qualified employee annuity, or a tax-sheltered annuity, and at the time the payments began, the beneficiary was either under age 75, or entitled to fewer than five years of guaranteed payment.

An annuity contract provides guaranteed payments if a minimum number of payments or a minimum amount is payable, even if the annuitant and any survivor annuitant do not live to receive the minimum. If the minimum amount is less than the total amount of the payments the annuitant is to receive, barring death, during the first five years after the payments begin the annuitant is entitled to fewer than five years of guaranteed payments. If an annuity starting date is after July 1, 1986, but the annuity does not meet all of the other conditions, the nonsimplified General Rule must be used. The nonsimplified General Rule must be used if annuity payments are from a nonqualified employee retirement plan.

Lump-Sum Distributions

If a lump-sum distribution is received from a qualified retirement plan, the holder may be able to elect optional methods to figure the tax on the distribution. A lump-sum distribution is paid within a single tax year. It is the distribution or payment of a plan participant's entire balance from all of the employer's qualified pension plans, from all of the employer's qualified stock bonus plans, or from all of the employer's qualified profit-sharing plans.

The distribution is paid:

1) Because of the plan participant's death.
2) After the participant reaches age 59 $1/_2$.
3) Because the participant, if an employee, separated from service.
4) After the participant, if a self-employed individual, becomes totally and permanently disabled.

Distributions that do not qualify as lump-sum distributions:

1) A distribution of the holder's deductible voluntary employee contributions and any net earnings on those contributions. A deductible voluntary employee contribution is a contribution that:
   a) Was made by the employee in a tax year beginning after 1981 and before 1987 to a qualified employer plan or a government plan that allows such contributions.
   b) Was not designated by the employee as nondeductible.
   c) Was not mandatory.

2) A U.S. Retirement Plan Bond distributed with a lump sum.
3) Any distribution made during the first five years that the employee was a participant in the plan, unless it was made because the employee died.
4) A distribution from an IRA.

5) A distribution of the redemption proceeds of bonds rolled over tax free to the plan from a qualified bond purchase plan.

6) A corrective distribution of excess deferrals, excess contributions, excess aggregate contributions, or excess annual additions.

7) A distribution from a tax-sheltered annuity.

8) A distribution from a privately purchased commercial annuity.

9) A distribution from a qualified plan if any part of the distribution is rolled over tax-free to another qualified plan or IRA.

10) A distribution from a deferred compensation plan of a state or from a local government or a tax-exempt organization.

FIVE- OR TEN-YEAR TAX OPTION

An annuitant can choose to use the five- or ten-year tax option or capital gain treatment only *once* after 1986 for any plan participant. The annuitant can recover his or her cost tax-free in a lump-sum distribution. The annuitant's cost consists of:

1) The plan participant's total nondeductible contributions to the plan.

2) The total of the plan participant's taxable costs of any life insurance contract distributed.

3) Any employer contributions that were taxable to the plan participant.

4) Repayments of loans that were taxable to the plan participant.

5) The net unrealized appreciation in employer's securities distributed.

6) The death benefit exclusion.

The total taxable amount of a lump-sum distribution is the part that is the employer's contribution and income earned on the holder's account.

The 20% capital gain election and the five- and ten-year tax options are special formulas used to figure a separate tax on a qualified lump-sum distribution only for the year in which the distribution is received. The tax is paid only once; the tax is not paid over the next five or ten years. This tax is in addition to the regular tax figured on the participant's other income. The use of either option can result in a smaller tax than the participant would pay by including the taxable amount of the distribution as ordinary income in figuring the regular tax.

Any individual, estate, or trust receiving a lump-sum distribution on behalf of a plan participant who was born before 1936 can use the five- or ten-year option. The plan participant who was 59 $1/_2$ in 1995 can, however, use the five-year tax option although he or she was born after 1935. This does not apply to the 10-year tax option.

Special Additional Taxes

To discourage the use of pension funds for purposes other than for normal retirement, the law imposes additional taxes on certain distribution of those funds. Ordinarily, the participant will not be subject to these taxes if he or she rolls over all distributions received, or begins drawing out the funds at normal retirement age and in reasonable amounts over the participant's life expectancy. The special additional taxes include taxes on:

1) Early distributions.

2) Excess distributions.

3) Excess accumulation by not taking the minimum required distributions.

Chapter 4
Corporate Taxes

FILING REQUIREMENTS

Each corporation, unless specifically exempt, must file a return even if it had no taxable income for the year and regardless of its gross income for the tax year. The income tax form for ordinary corporations is Form 1120. A corporation does not have to file an income tax return if it has dissolved, but may have to file a return for any year following the year in which it dissolved if it carries on substantial activities. A corporation has dissolved if it has ceased business and has neither assets nor income. The collection of assets or payment of obligations in the termination of its business affairs is considered substantial activity. A corporation must file even if it has stopped doing business and disposed of all of its assets, except for a small sum of cash retained to pay state taxes to keep its corporate charter.

SMALL CORPORATIONS

Certain small corporations can file Form 1120-A to report taxable income if the corporation meets the following requirements:

1) Its gross receipts are under $500,000.
2) Its total income is under $500,000.
3) It does not have ownership in a foreign corporation.

47

4) It does not have foreign shareholders who own, directly or indirectly, 50% or more of its stock.

5) It is not a member of a controlled group.

6) It is not a personal holding company.

7) It is not a consolidated corporate return filer.

8) It is not a corporation undergoing a dissolution or liquidation.

9) It is not filing its final tax return.

10) Its only dividend income, none of which represents debt-financed securities, is from domestic corporations and those dividends qualify for the 70% deduction.

11) It has no nonrefundable tax credits other than the general business credit and the credit for prior-year minimum tax.

12) It is not subject to environmental tax.

13) It has no liability for interest on certain installment sales of timeshares and residential lots, or interest on deferred tax liability or installment payment of taxes.

14) It has no liability for interest due under the look-back method or on completion of a long-term contract.

15) It is not required to file Form 8621.

16) It has no liability for tax on a nonqualified withdrawal from a capital construction fund.

17) It is not making an election to forego the carryback period of an NOL.

18) It is not electing to pay tax on a gain from the sale of an intangible.

19) It is not an organization such as an S corporation, life or mutual insurance company, or political organization, required to file a specialized form.

EXTENSION OF TIME TO FILE

A corporation will receive an automatic six-month extension of time for filing its return by submitting an application for extension on form 7004. The form is filed with the IRS service center where the corporation will file its income tax return. The IRS can terminate an extension at any time by mailing a notice of termination to the corporation. Any automatic extension of time for filing a corporation income tax return will not extend the time for paying the tax due on the return. The tax is deposited with Form 7994 using Form 8109. If the tax reported on Form 7004 is less than the actual tax due, interest is charged on the difference.

A corporation files its income tax return in the IRS service center in the area serving the location of the corporation's principal office for keeping its books and records. The separate income tax returns of a group of corporations located in several service center regions can be filed with the service center for the area in which the principal office of the managing corporation which keeps all the books and records is located. Income tax deposits are made either to an authorized financial institution, or to a Federal Reserve Bank. All deposits are made with Form 8109.

PENALTIES

If a corporation does not file its income taxes by the due date—including extensions—and it cannot show reasonable cause, a delinquency penalty for the amount of the underpayment will apply. An *underpayment* is the excess of the required tax amount over the tax deposited by the due date. The tax due is the tax liability that would be shown on a return, less credits and any tax payments made before the due date. The penalty is figured by multiplying the underpayment by one of the following percentages:

1) 2% if deposited by the fifth day after the deposit due date.
2) 5% if deposited after the fifth day, but by the 15th day after the deposit due date.
3) 10% if deposited after the 15th day after the deposit due date.

The percentage is 15% if the tax is not deposited by the earlier of:

1) The day that is 10 days after the date of the first delinquency notice to the corporation.
2) The day on which notice and demand for immediate payment is given.

If the return is not filed within 60 days of the due date, including extensions, the penalty for failure to file is at least $100, or the balance of tax due, whichever is less, until reasonable cause is shown. The penalty does not apply to estimated taxes.

REASONABLE CAUSE

A taxpayer must show *reasonable cause* to avoid a penalty for a failure to file a tax return, pay the taxes, or deposit taxes by filing a statement of the facts establishing reasonable cause for the failure with the service center where the corporation files its return. The statement must contain a declaration that it was made under the penalties of perjury. Payments made after the due date are subject to an interest charge, even if filing extensions were granted. Payments of taxes, other than estimated tax payments, made after the due date can also be subject to a penalty of 0.5% a month or part of a month up to a maximum of 25%. In certain situations, the penalty will increase to 1% a month, or part of a month, up to a maximum of 25%.

Recovery Penalty

A person who is responsible for withholding, accounting for, depositing, or paying withholding taxes, and willfully fails to do so, can be held liable for a penalty equal to the tax not paid, plus interest. A responsible person can be an officer of a corporation, a partner, a sole proprietor, or an employee of any form of business. An agent or trustee with authority over the funds of a business can also be held responsible for a penalty. *Willfully* means voluntarily, consciously, and intentionally. Paying other business expenses instead of taxes is considered to be acting willfully. The person responsible for the collection and payment of withholding taxes can be subject to a penalty even though he or she is an officer or employee of a corporation, or a member or employee of a partnership. There are other civil penalties that can apply because of negligence, substantial understatement of tax, and fraud. Criminal penalties apply to willful failure to file, tax evasion, or making a false statement.

Capital Contributions, Retained Earnings

Contributions to the capital of a corporation, whether or not by shareholders, are *paid-in capital*. However, contributions to a corporation to aid construction activities, or another contribution as a customer or potential customer is taxable to the corporation. The basis of property contributed by a person other than a shareholder is zero. If a corporation receives a cash contribution from a person other than a shareholder, the *basis* of property acquired with the money, during the 12-month period beginning on the day it is received the contribution, is reduced by the amount of the contribution. If the amount contributed is more than the cost of the property acquired, the basis is reduced, but not below zero, of the other properties held by the corporation on the last day of the 12-month period in the following order:

1) Depreciable property.
2) Amortizable property.
3) Property subject to cost depletion, but not to percentage depletion.
4) All other remaining properties.

The basis of property in a category is reduced to zero before going to the next category.

There may be more than one piece of property in each category. The reduction of the basis of each property is based on the ratio of the basis of each piece of property to the total basis of all property in that category. If the corporation wishes to make the adjustment in some other way, it must get IRS consent. The corporation must file a request for consent with its income tax return for the tax year in which it receives the contribution.

ACCUMULATED RETAINED EARNINGS

A corporation can accumulate its earnings for a possible expansion or for other bona fide business reasons. However, if a corporation allows earnings to accumulate beyond the *reasonable needs* of the business, it can be subject to an *accumulated earnings* tax of 39.8%. If the accumulated earnings tax applies, interest applies to an underpayment of taxes from the date the corporate return was originally due, without extensions. The tax applies regardless of the number of shareholders.

An accumulation of $250,000 or less is within the reasonable needs of a business. An accumulation of $150,000 or less is within the reasonable needs of a business whose principal function is performing services in the fields of health, law, engineering, architecture, accounting, actuarial science, veterinary services, performing arts, and consulting. In determining if a corporation has accumulated earnings and profits beyond its reasonable needs, the listed and readily marketable securities owned by the corporation and purchased with its earnings and profits are valued at net liquidation value, not at cost.

The reasonable needs of a business include:

1) Specific, definite, and feasible plans for use of the earnings accumulation in the business.

2) The amount necessary to redeem the corporation's stock included in a deceased shareholder's gross estate.

3) The amount that does not exceed the reasonably anticipated total estate and inheritance taxes, and funeral and administration expenses incurred by the shareholder's estate.

If a corporation with accumulated earnings of more than $250,000 does not make regular distributions to its shareholders, it should be prepared to show a bona fide business reason for not doing so. For a corporation to avoid liability for accumulated earnings tax, it must show that tax avoidance by its shareholders is not one of the purposes for the accumulation; the simple existence of a tax avoidance purpose is sufficient for imposing the accumulated earnings tax.

DISTRIBUTIONS

Corporate distributions include ordinary dividends, stock dividends, or a return of capital, and can be made in property as well as in distributions of money. Any distribution to shareholders from earnings and profits is a *dividend*. A distribution is not a taxable dividend if it is a return of capital to the shareholders. Most dividends are paid in money, but they can also be in stock or other property. A corporation must file a Form 1099-DIV for each shareholder to whom a corporation pays gross dividends of $10 or more during a calendar year, and the corporation files a Form 1096 to summarize and transmit the Forms 1099-DIV, and Form 5452 if the corporation pays dividends that are not taxable. The corporation can furnish Forms 1099-DIV to shareholders after November 30 of the year of payment, but not before the final payment for the year. This information must be furnished by January 31 of the year following the close of the calendar year during which the corporation makes the payments.

For certain shareholders, the IRS can require a corporation to keep a *backup withholding* equal to 31% of the dividends paid to that shareholder, and a 1099 DIV form must be filed regardless of the amount of the dividend. Backup withholding is for payments of interest, dividends, patronage dividends, rents, royalties, commissions, nonemployees' compensation, and other payments made in the course of a taxpayer's trade or business. Real estate transactions and canceled debts are not subject to backup withholding. If the payment is a reportable interest, dividend, or other payment, backup withholding applies if:

1) The payee does not furnish a taxpayer identification number (TIN) to the payer.
2) The IRS notifies the payer to impose backup withholding because the payee furnished an incorrect TIN.
3) The payer is notified that the payee is subject to backup withholding.
4) For interest and dividend accounts opened, or instruments acquired, the payee does not notify the payer under penalties of perjury, that he or she is not subject to backup withholding under item 3.
5) For interest, dividend, broker, or barter exchange accounts, the payee does not certify to the payer, under penalties of perjury, the TIN furnished by the payee is correct.

The payee can use taxpayer identification number only to comply with tax laws. If the taxpayer identification number, including Social Security number, is disclosed in violation of federal law, the payer will be liable for criminal penalties and civil damages.

The amount of a distribution paid to any shareholder is the money paid plus the fair market value (FMV) on the distribution date of other property transferred to the shareholder. The distribution of the liabilities of the corporation assumed by the shareholder are reduced, but not below zero, and by liabilities to which the property is subject. The basis of property received that he or she holds is the FMV.

Property means any property including money, securities, and indebtedness to the corporation, except stock of the distributing corporation or rights to acquire such stock. If the FMV on the date of the sale or exchange exceeds the price paid by the shareholder that is not a corporation, the excess is a distribution. If a corporation cancels a shareholder's debt without repayment by the shareholder, the amount canceled is treated as a distribution to the shareholder.

A distribution by a corporation not in complete liquidation does not recognize gain or loss on property distributed to shareholders. If a corporation distributes property, other than its own obligations, to a shareholder, and the property's FMV exceeds the corporation's adjusted basis, the property is treated as sold at the time of distribution. The corporation recognizes a gain on the excess of the FMV over the adjusted basis of the property. If the FMV of depreciated property distributed to shareholders is more than the adjusted basis of that property, the corporation must report ordinary income because of depreciation. This applies even though the distribution, either as a dividend or in liquidation, might otherwise be nontaxable.

TAXABLE STATUS OF A DISTRIBUTION

The part of a distribution from either current or accumulated earnings and profits is a dividend. The part of the distribution that is more than earnings and profits reduces the adjusted basis of the stock in the hands of the shareholder. Any amount that exceeds the adjusted basis of the stock is treated by the shareholder as gain from the sale or exchange of property and is usually a capital gain. Whether a distribution is a taxable dividend to the shareholders, used to reduce the adjusted basis of their stock, or treated as gain from the sale of property, depends upon whether the distribution is *more* than:

1) Earnings and profits for the tax year of the distribution figured as of the close of that year without reduction for any distribution during the year, plus
2) Accumulated earnings and profits.

The current earnings and profits at the time of a distribution do not necessarily determine whether the distribution is a taxable dividend. If there is a deficit in earnings and profits for the tax year of the distribution, the taxable status of the distribution depends on the amount of accumulated earnings and profits. In determining accumulated earnings and profits, the deficit is pro-rated in earnings and profits for the current year to the dates of distributions.

NONTAXABLE DIVIDENDS

Nontaxable dividends are distributions to shareholders on their stock in the ordinary course of business. They are not taxable as dividends because the amount of the distributions is greater than the corporation's earnings and profits. Attach Form 5452 to the corporate return if nontaxable dividends are paid to shareholders.

ADJUSTMENT TO EARNINGS AND PROFITS

For a cash distribution, the current earnings and profits are decreased by the amount distributed, but not below zero. For a distribution of an obligation of the distributing corporation, the earnings and profits are decreased by the principal amount of the obligation, but not below zero. For the distribution of an original issue discount obligation, earnings and profits are decreased by the total issue price of the obligation, but not below zero. For a distribution of other property, the earnings and profits are decreased by the adjusted basis of the property, but not below zero. For a distribution of appreciated property, other than the corporation's obligations, the earnings and profits are increased by the excess of the FMV over the adjusted basis of the property. The earnings and profits are decreased, but not below zero, by the FMV of the appreciated property, and also by the FMV instead of by the adjusted basis of other property. The decrease in earnings and profits by the FMV of distributed property is reduced for any liability to which the distributive property is subject, and any liability assumed by the shareholder in connection with the distribution.

DISTRIBUTION OF STOCK AND STOCK RIGHTS

A shareholder does not include a distribution of stock or rights to acquire stock in a corporation in gross income unless it is one of the following:

1) A distribution instead of money or other property.
2) A disproportionate distribution.
3) A distribution of preferred stock.

4) A distribution of common and preferred stock, unless the corporation can establish to the satisfaction of the IRS that the distribution will not result in a disproportionate distribution.

5) A distribution of common and preferred stock resulting in the receipt of preferred stock by some common shareholders and receipt of common stock by other common shareholders.

Even if the distribution falls into one of these five categories, there must be sufficient earnings and profits for the distribution to be a dividend. If the distribution does not fall into one of these categories, the corporation does not adjust its earnings and profits.

A distribution is instead of money or other property if any shareholders have an election to get either stock, rights to acquire stock, money, or property. This applies regardless of whether:

1) The distribution is actually made in whole or in part in stock or in stock rights.

2) The election or option is exercised or exercisable before or after the declaration of the distribution.

3) The declaration of the distribution provides that it will be made in one type unless the shareholder specifically requests payment in the other.

4) The election governing the nature of the distribution is provided in the declaration of the distribution, corporate charter, or arises from the circumstances of the distribution.

5) All or part of the shareholders have the election.

If the common shareholders receive a pro rata distribution of preferred stock with an option to redeem it for money immediately, the distribution is instead of money. The shareholders include the distribution in gross income.

A distribution is disproportionate if some shareholders receive cash or other property and other shareholders receive increased proportionate interests in the assets or earnings and profits of the corporation.

Shareholders are not required to receive the cash or property by means of a distribution or series of distributions as long as the result is that they did receive it in their capacity as shareholders and that the distribution is one which would be subject to the rules that apply to the taxing of dividends. In order for a distribution of stock to be considered as one of a series of distributions, it is not necessary that it be pursuant to a plan to distribute cash or property to some shareholders and to increase the proportionate interests of other shareholders. It is sufficient if there is either an actual or deemed distribution of stock and, as a result of it, some shareholders increase their proportionate interests.

TRANSFER OF STOCK TO CREDITORS

If a corporation transfers its stock in satisfaction of indebtedness, and the market value of the stock is less than the indebtedness it owes, the corporation has income to the extent of the difference from the cancellation of indebtedness. A corporation can exclude all or a portion of the income created by the stock for debt transfer if it is in a bankruptcy proceeding or, if it is not in bankruptcy proceeding, it can exclude the income to the extent it is insolvent. However, the corporation must reduce its attributes, to the extent it has any, by the amount of excluded income. A corporation does not realize income because of stock for debt exchange if it is in bankruptcy, or to the extent it is insolvent. Consequently, there is no gross income to exclude and no deduction of its tax attributes is necessary. This exception applies to stock transferred in satisfaction of its debt.

GOLDEN PARACHUTE PAYMENTS

Corporations can enter into golden parachute contracts with key personnel. Under a typical golden parachute contract, the corporation agrees to make payments to certain officers, shareholders, or highly compensated individuals when considered necessary by certain events that may occur. The contract provides for payment when there is:

1) A change in ownership or control of the corporation.
2) A change in the ownership of a substantial part of the corporation's assets.

The corporation's deduction is limited if the total present value of the payments to any officer, shareholder, or highly compensated individual equals or exceeds three times the recipient's *base amount*. The base amount of a recipient is the average annualized includable compensation that was payable to the recipient by the corporation during the five tax years ending before the date of the change in ownership or control. It cannot deduct the excess of any parachute payment over the part of the base amount allocated to the payment. The law allows a nondeductible excise tax on the recipient of 30% of these payments in addition to the regular income tax.

CAPITAL LOSSES

A corporation, other than an S corporation, can deduct capital losses only up to its capital gains. If a corporation has a net capital loss, it cannot deduct the loss in the current tax year. It carries the loss to other tax years and deducts it from capital gains that occur in those years. A net capital loss can be carried back three years and deducted from any total net capital gain which occurred in that year. It carries the loss to other tax years and deducts it from capital gains that occur in those years. When a net capital loss is carried to another tax year, it is treated as a short-term loss; it does not retain its original identity as long-term or short-term.

When carrying capital loss from one year to another, the following rules apply:

1) When figuring this year's net capital loss, no capital loss carried from another year can be used. Capital losses can be carried only to years that would otherwise have a total net capital gain.

2) If capital losses are carried from two or more years to the same year, the loss is deducted from the earliest year first. When that loss is fully deducted, the loss is deducted from the next earliest year, and so on.

3) A capital loss that is carried from another year to produce or increase a net operating loss in the year to which it is carried cannot be used.

ALTERNATIVE MINIMUM TAX (AMT)

The tax laws give special treatment to certain kinds of income and allow special deductions and credits for certain kinds of expenses. In order that taxpayers who benefit from these laws will pay at least a minimum amount of tax, a special tax was enacted, the *alternative minimum tax (AMT)* for corporations. The AMT rate for corporations is 20%. There is an exemption of up to $40,000. This amount is reduced by 25% of the amount by which AMTI (alternative minimum taxable income) exceeds $150,000. A minimum tax credit can be applied against a regular tax liability in later years for the AMT caused by certain preferences and adjustments.

AMT is calculated by making certain adjustments to the taxable income on the tax return. The adjustments, termed *tax adjustments and preferences,* eliminate the tax advantages of certain items that receive preferential tax treatment. The adjustment for these items is the difference between the recomputed item for AMT purposes and the amount on the return. There can be either increases or decreases entered as negative amounts. If an expense or loss claimed for regular tax purposes is more than the recomputed AMT expense or loss, the difference is an increase in taxable income. If the expense or loss is less than the recomputed AMT expense or loss, the difference is a decrease in taxable income.

The adjustment for accelerated depreciation on property applies to property placed in service after 1986. The depreciation deduction used for AMT is the amount calculated using the alternative depreciation system (ADS) under the MACRO system. For real property, the straight-line method with a 40-year recovery period is used. For property other than real property, the 150% declining balance method is used, switching to the straight-line method when it gives a larger allowance. This adjustment applies to property placed in service after 1986. It also applies to property placed in service after July 31, 1986, and before 1987, if the taxpayer elected to use MACRO.

The following types of property are not considered in figuring this adjustment item:

1) Property that is excluded from MACRO that is depreciated under the unit-of-production method.

2) Certain public utility property.

3) Any motion picture film or video tape.

4) Any sound recording.

The adjustment is the difference between the total depreciation for all property for AMT purposes and the total depreciation for regular income tax purposes. The effect of using two different types of depreciation—one for regular income tax and one for the AMT—is that a corporation will have a different basis in the property for the AMT. For property placed in service before 1987, accelerated depreciation is a preference item and must continue to be treated as a preference item.

Chapter 5
Business Expenses

To be deductible, a business expense must be both ordinary and necessary. An expense does not have to be indispensable to be considered necessary. It is important to separate business expenses from the expenses used to figure the cost of goods sold and capital expenses.

Business expenses must be kept separate from personal expenses. If an expense is partly for business and partly personal, separate the personal part from the business part.

Adjusted Basis

Before figuring the gain or loss on a sale, exchange, or other disposition of property, or figuring allowable depreciation, depletion, or amortization, certain adjustments must be made which increase or decrease the basis of the property. The result of these adjustments to the basis is the *adjusted basis*.

Increases to the Basis

The basis of any property should be increased by all items properly added to a capital account. This includes the cost of any improvements having a useful life of more than one year and amounts spent after a casualty to restore the damaged property. Rehabilitation expenses also increase the basis. However, any rehabilitation credit allowed for those expenses must be subtracted before they are added to the basis. If any of the credit has to be recaptured, the basis is increased by the amount of the recapture.

If additions or improvements are made to business property, separate accounts should be kept for them. Also, the basis of each addition should be kept according to the depreciation rules in effect when the addition or improvement is placed in service.

Some items that add to the basis of property are:

1) The cost of extending utility service lines to the property.
2) Legal fees, such as the cost of defending and protecting a title.
3) Legal fees for obtaining a decrease in an assessment levied against property to pay for local improvements.
4) Zoning costs.
5) The capitalized value of redeemable rent.

Assessments are added for such improvements as streets and sidewalks which increase the value of the property assessed to the basis of the property. These assessments cannot be deducted as taxes, but assessments can be deducted for maintenance or repair or for meeting interest charges on the improvements.

DECREASES TO THE BASIS

Some items that reduce the basis of property are:

1) The deduction for clean fuel vehicles and clean fuel vehicle refueling property.
2) Nontaxable corporate distributions.
3) Deductions previously allowed, or allowable, for amortization, depreciation, and depletion.
4) Exclusion from income of subsidies for energy conservation measures.
5) Credit for qualified electric vehicles.
6) Gain from the sale of old homes on which taxes were postponed.
7) Investment credit.
8) Casualty and theft losses.
9) Canceled debt excluded from income.
10) Rebates received from a manufacturer or seller.
11) Easements.
12) Residential energy credit.
13) Gas-guzzler tax.

14) Tax credit or refund for buying a diesel powered highway vehicle.

15) Nontaxable corporate distributions.

AMORTIZATION

If the business is organized as a partnership or corporation, only the partnership or corporation can elect to amortize the start-up or organization costs. Neither a partner nor shareholder can make this election. If a partner or shareholder incurs costs in setting up a partnership or corporation, neither can amortize them. If the partnership or corporation does not reimburse a partner or shareholder for these costs, it cannot amortize them. These costs then become part of the basis of the interest in the business; they can be recovered only when a partner or shareholder sells his or her interest in the partnership or corporation. However, an individual can elect to amortize the costs incurred to investigate an interest in an existing partnership. These costs qualify as business start-up costs if either he or she succeeded in acquiring an interest.

HOW TO AMORTIZE

Start-up and organizational costs must be deducted in equal amounts over a period of 60 months, or more. The period elected for start-up costs can be different from the period elected for organizational costs, as long as both are 60 months or more. Once an amortization period is chosen, it cannot be changed.

To figure deductions, total start-up or organizational costs are divided by the months in the amortization period. The result is the amount that can be deducted each month. However, partnerships on the cash method of accounting are not allowed a deduction for an expense that has not been paid by the end of the tax year. Any expense that the partnership could have deducted as an organizational expense in an earlier year, if it had been paid, can be deducted in the tax year of payment.

The amortization period starts with the month that business operations begins. Amortization can start only when the partnership actually goes into business. For the amortization of organizational costs, a partnership or corporation is considered to begin business operations when it starts the activities for which it is organized. This can happen either before or after the corporate charter is granted or a partnership agreement is signed. A partnership or corporation is considered to begin business when its activities have reached the point where the nature of its business operations is establish. The acquisition of the assets to operate a business constitutes the beginning of business activities.

Construction Period Interest and Taxes

The cost of constructing or improving property used in a trade or business or an activity engaged in for-profit must be capitalized. These capitalized costs, including construction period interest and taxes incurred after 1986, generally are recovered through depreciation. However, construction period interest and taxes incurred before 1987 on real property, other than low-income housing, expected to be used for a trade or business or in an activity conducted for profit, generally cannot be depreciated. Instead, the amounts usually have to be amortized.

The amortization year means the tax year in which the amount was paid or accrued, and each tax year thereafter starting with the later of:

1) The tax year after the tax year in which the amount was paid or accrued, or
2) The tax year in which the real property was ready to be placed in service or held for sale, until the full amount has been allowed as a deduction, or until the property is sold or exchanged.

Research and Experimental Costs

Research and experimental costs can be either amortized or deducted as current business costs. The costs of research and experimentation are generally capital expenses. However, these costs can be deducted as current business expenses. The choice applies to all research and experimental costs; some of these expenses can be deducted and others capitalized. However, if the choice is not to deduct research and experimental costs currently, there are other choices. They can be treated as deferred expenses and amortized over a period of at least 60 months, beginning with the month that an economic benefit is received from the research. The expenditures can also be deducted over a 10-year period beginning with the tax year they were paid or incurred.

Research and development costs are reasonable costs incurred in a trade or business that are the experimental or laboratory portion of research and development costs. This includes all costs incident to the development or improvement of a product. It also includes the cost to obtain a patent, such as attorney's fees in making and perfecting a patent application. Costs qualify as research or experimental costs, depending on the nature of the activity the costs relate to, rather than the nature of the product or the improvement being developed, or the level of technological advancement represented.

Qualifying costs are the experimental or laboratory portion of research and development costs that are for activities intended to discover information that would eliminate uncertainty concerning the development or improvement of a product. Uncertainty exists if the information available does not establish the capability or method for developing or improving the product or the appropriate design of the product.

Research and experimental costs do not include expenses for:

1) Quality control testing.
2) Efficiency surveys.
3) Management studies.
4) Consumer surveys.
5) Advertising or promotions.
6) The acquisition of another's patent, model, production, or process.
7) Research in connection with literary, historical, or similar projects.

The term *product* includes:

1) Any pilot model.
2) Process.
3) Formula.
4) Invention.
5) Technique.
6) Similar property.

The term also includes products used in the trade or business or held for sale, lease, or license. To choose to deduct research and experimental costs currently, they should be claimed as an expense deduction on the income tax return for the year in which they are first incurred. If the choice is made after the first year, permission must be obtained from the IRS. The business may qualify for a credit on some or all of the research and experiment costs no matter how they are treated. The amount deducted or capitalized must be reduced by the amount of the credit, unless a reduced credit is taken. The research credit applies to expenses paid or incurred before June 30, 1995.

ACCOUNTABLE PLAN

To be an accountable plan, the reimbursement or allowance arrangements must meet *qualifying arrangements*. To qualify as an accountable plan, the reimbursement or allowance arrangement must require the employees to meet *all* of the following rules:

1) The employees must have paid or incurred deductible expenses while performing services as employees of the business.
2) The employees must adequately account to the employer for these expenses within a reasonable period of time.
3) Employees must return any excessive reimbursements or allowances within a reasonable period of time.

If any expenses reimbursed under this arrangement are not substantiated, or are an excess reimbursement that is not returned within a reasonable period of time by an employee, the expenses cannot be treated as reimbursed under an accountable plan; they must be treated under a nonaccountable plan. *A reasonable period of time* depends on the acts and circumstances. It can be considered reasonable if employees adequately account for expenses within 60 days after they were paid or incurred and if any excess reimbursement is returned within 120 days after the expense was paid or incurred. It is also considered reasonable if the employees are given a periodic statement, at least quarterly, that asks the employees to either return or adequately account for outstanding amounts within 120 days.

NONACCOUNTABLE PLAN

A nonaccountable plan is a reimbursement or expense allowance arrangement that does not meet the three rules listed above. In addition, the following payments made under an accountable plan will be treated as being paid under a nonaccountable plan:

1) Excess reimbursements the employee failed to return to the employer.
2) Reimbursement of nondeductible expenses related to the employer's business.

An arrangement that repays an employee for business expenses by reducing the amount reported as wages, salary, or other compensation will be treated as a nonaccountable plan. This is because the employee is entitled to receive the full amount of his or her compensation regardless of whether any business expenses were incurred. The employer will combine the amount of any reimbursement or other expense allowance paid under a nonaccountable plan with the employee's wages, salary, or other compensation. If expenses are reimbursed under an otherwise accountable plan and not returned within a reasonable period of time, the amount of any reimbursement that was not adequately accounted for is considered as paid under a nonaccountable plan. The remainder is treated as having been paid under an accountable plan.

REIMBURSEMENTS

How a deduction, reimbursement, or allowance, including per diem allowances, is made for travel, meals, and entertainment expenses incurred by employees depends on whether the business uses an accountable plan or a nonaccountable plan. If expenses are reimbursed under an *accountable plan*, they are deducted as travel, meal, and entertainment expenses. If the expenses are reimbursed under a *nonaccountable plan,* the reimbursements must be reported as wages, and the employer deducts them as wages.

Under an accountable plan, the business can take a deduction for expenses if the employees are reimbursed for these expenses. The amount reimbursed for meals and entertainment are subject to the 50% deduction limit. For employee travel, meals, and entertainment expenses reimbursed under a nonaccountable plan, the reimbursement is subject to income tax withholding, social security, Medicare, and federal unemployment taxes. The reimbursement as compensation or wages can be deducted to the extent it meets the deductibility tests for employees' pay.

EXCESS REIMBURSEMENT OR ALLOWANCE

An excess reimbursement or allowance is any amount an employee is paid that is more than the business-related expenses that the employee adequately accounted for to his or her employer. The definition of a *reasonable period of time* depends on the facts of the employee's situation. The IRS considers it reasonable for an employee to:

1) Receive an advance within 30 days of the time the expense has been incurred.

2) Adequately account for expenses within 60 days after they were paid or incurred.

3) Return any excess reimbursement within 120 days after the expense was paid or incurred.

If the employee is given periodic statements (at least quarterly) that ask for either a return or an adequate account for outstanding advances, and the employee complies within 120 days of the statement, the amount will be considered accounted for or returned within a reasonable period of time. If the employee meets the three rules for accountable plans, an employer should not include any reimbursements in the employee's income. If the expenses equal the employee's reimbursement, the employee has no deduction since the expenses and reimbursement are equal.

If an employee's expenses are reimbursed under an otherwise accountable plan, but the employee does not return within a reasonable period of time any reimbursement for which he or she did not adequately account, then only the amount for which the employee did adequately account is considered as paid under an accountable plan. The remaining expenses are treated as having been reimbursed under a nonaccountable plan. If an employee is reimbursed under an employer's accountable plan for expenses related to the employer's business, some of which are deductible as employee business expenses and some of which are not deductible, the reimbursements received for the nondeductible expenses are treated as paid under a nonaccountable plan.

Per Diem Allowance

Under an accountable plan, employees can be reimbursed based on travel days, miles, or some other fixed allowance. In these cases, the employee is considered to have accounted to his or her employer if the payments do not exceed rates established by the federal government. If the per diem paid exceeds the federal rate, the excess amount must be reported as wages. If employers reimburse employees with a per diem allowance, two facts affect how the employer reports and deducts the reimbursement:

1) The federal rate for the area where an employee traveled.
2) Whether the allowance is more than the federal rate.

The federal rate can be figured by using the regular federal per diem rate. The *regular federal per diem rate* is the highest amount that the federal government will pay to its employees for lodging, meals, and incidental expenses while they are traveling away from home in a particular area. The rates are different for different locations in the country and can be obtained from the IRS.

Applying the Limit

The 50% limit on the deduction for meal and entertainment expenses reimbursed to employees under an accountable plan applies if the expense is otherwise a permissible deduction. The limit applies to trade or business expenses and to expenses incurred for the production of income including rental or royalty income.

The 50% limit applies to reimbursement made to employees for expenses they incur while traveling away from home on business and for entertaining business customers at a restaurant. It applies to attending a business convention or reception, business meeting, or business luncheon at a club. The deduction limit may also apply to meals furnished to employees on the employer's premises. The limit does not apply to other services, such as transportation to and from the activity, or to lodging.

Automobile Expenses

1996 Luxury Automobile Limits. The 1996 limits applicable to depreciation of luxury automobiles remain unchanged from 1995. The 1996 depreciation limit, therefore, are first year, $3,060; second year, $4,900; third year, $2,950; subsequent years, $1,775. The leased automobile inclusion amounts for 1996 actually are lower than for automobiles first leased in 1995, probably due to a drop in the rate of return the IRS compares to an inflation quotient when determining these amounts.

A choice must be made whether to deduct car expenses by claiming the standard mileage rate or using actual expenses. In either case, it is important to keep accurate and detailed records of the business use of a car. When an employer provides an employee with a car, the employee can deduct the actual expenses of operating the car for business purposes. The amount deductible depends on the amount that the employer included in the employee's income and the business and personal miles driven during the year. The standard mileage *cannot be used* for a car the employee does not own. The employer can report either the actual value of the employee's use of the car or the value of the car as if the employee used it entirely for personal purposes, which is a 100% income inclusion. The employer is required to state the amount if 100% of the annual lease value was included in the employee's income. The employee can deduct the value of the business use of an employer-provided car if the employer reported 100% of the value of the car in the employee's income.

If less than the full annual lease value of the car was included on a Form W-2, this means that the employee only includes the value for his or her personal use of the car. The value should not be entered on the Form 2106EZ because it is not deductible. If the employee paid any actual costs to operate the car that were not reimbursed by the employer, the business portion of the costs can be deducted. (The costs are usually for gasoline, oil, and repairs.)

A reimbursement or other expense allowance arrangement is a system or plan that an employer uses to pay, substantiate, and recover the expenses, advances, and amounts charged to the employer for employee business expenses. A system can also be used to keep track of amounts an employee receives from the employer's agent, or a third party. Arrangements include mileage allowances. If a single payment included both wages and an expense reimbursement, the amount of the reimbursement must be specifically identified.

An employer can use different options for reimbursing an employee for business-related car expenses. The employer can reimburse an employee:

1) For actual expenses.
2) At the standard mileage rate.
3) At a fair rate or stated schedule.
4) By any other method that is approved by the IRS.

A mileage allowance paid at a flat rate or stated schedule can be paid periodically at a fixed rate, at a cents-per-mile rate, at a variable rate based on a stated schedule, or any combination of these rates. The employer should tell the employee what method of reimbursement is used and what records the employee must submit. If the employee is paid a salary or commission with the understanding that he or she will pay his or her own expenses, then the employee will not be reimbursed or given an allowance for expenses. In this situation the employee has no reimbursement or allowance arrangement, and deducts expenses.

CAR OR MILEAGE ALLOWANCES

How a car or mileage allowance is received under an accountable plan depends on whether the allowance was more than the standard mileage rate. If an allowance is *less than or equal* to the standard mileage rate, the related expenses or the car mileage allowance need not be reported on his or her tax return. If the employee's actual expenses or the standard mileage rate are *more than* the car mileage allowance, the excess amount is deductible. If actual expenses are deducted on the return, the employee must prove to the IRS the total amount of the expenses and reimbursements.

WHAT IS ADEQUATE ACCOUNTING?

To qualify for an accountable plan, an employee must adequately account to his or her employer for incurred expenses. The employee adequately accounts by giving the employer documentary evidence of the mileage or other car expenses, along with a statement of expenses, an account book, a diary, or a similar record in which is entered the mileage of each expense at or near the time the expense was paid. Documentary evidence includes receipts, canceled checks, bills, and invoices. An employee must account for all amounts received from his or her employer during the year as either advance reimbursements, or as allowances for business use of the employee's car. This includes amounts that were charged to the employer by credit card or other method. The employer must be given the same type of records and supporting information that would have to be given to the IRS if the IRS questioned a deduction on his or her return. The amount must be paid back for reimbursement or other expense allowances which are not adequately accounted for, or for the amount that exceeds the amount which was adequately accounted for. A car or mileage allowance satisfies the adequate accounting requirements if:

1) The employer reasonably limits payments of the car expenses to those that are ordinary and necessary in the conduct of trade or business.

2) The allowance is paid at the standard mileage rate, at another rate per mile, or based on a fixed and variable rate (FAVR) allowance.

3) The employee proves to the employer, within a reasonable period of time, the dates, place, and business purpose of using his or her car.

Additional recordkeeping requirements must be met if the employee is related to his or her employer. If related to the employer, the employee must be able to prove expenses to the IRS even if the expenses have been adequately accounted for to the employer, and that the employee has returned any excess reimbursement, which can include using either the standard mileage rate, or a FAVR allowance. An employee is considered related to his or her employer if:

1) The employer is an employee's brother, sister, half-brother or half-sister, spouse, ancestor, or lineal descendant.

2) The employer is a corporation in which the employee owns, directly or indirectly, more than 10% in value of the outstanding stock.

3) Certain fiduciary relationships exist between the employee and the employer involving grantors, trusts, and beneficiaries.

Stock is considered to be indirectly owned if the employee has an interest in a corporation, partnership, estate, or trust that owns the stock, or if a family member or partner owns the stock.

PROVING A CAR OR MILEAGE ALLOWANCE

If an employer pays for an employee's expenses using a car or mileage allowance, the employee can use the allowance as proof for the amount of the expenses. The amount of expense that can be proven cannot be more than the standard mileage rate, or the amount of the FAVR allowance. Only the amount can be proven under the adequate accounting requirements. The employee must still prove the dates, place, and business purpose for each expense. An employee can prove the amount of expenses if the employer reimburses car expenses at a fixed rate, at a cents-per-mile rate, or at a variable rate based on a stated schedule which cannot exceed the standard mileage rate.

The employer can choose to reimburse car expenses by paying an allowance that includes a combination of payments covering fixed and variable costs, such as a cents-per-mile rate to cover variable operating costs, plus a flat amount to cover fixed costs such as depreciation, insurance, and other expenses. This is called a FAVR allowance. If the employer chooses to use this method, he or she will request the necessary records from the employee and will not include any part considered to be paid from an accountable plan on the employee's Form W-2. The IRS will consider the employee to have proven the amount reimbursed by the employer.

Under an accountable plan, an employee must return any excess reimbursement or other expense allowance for business car expenses to the person paying the reimbursement or allowance. *Excess reimbursement* means any amount for which the employee did not adequately account within a reasonable period of time.

Chapter 6
Federal Tax Aspects of Bankruptcy

This chapter covers the federal income tax for the bankruptcy of corporations, partnerships, and for individuals. The discussion does not provide detailed coverage of the tax rules for complex corporate bankruptcy reorganizations, or other highly technical and legal aspects of business and individual bankruptcy proceedings. Competent professional advice should be obtained for the highly complex bankruptcy law.

Bankruptcy proceedings begin with the filing of a petition with the bankruptcy court. The filing of the petition creates a bankruptcy estate, which consists of all the assets of the *person* filing the bankruptcy petition.

Note: A *person* in the tax law is an individual, a trust, estate, partnership, association, company, corporation, an officer or employee of a corporation, or a member or employee of a partnership who is under a duty to surrender the property or rights to property to discharge the obligation. The term *person* also includes an officer or employee of the United States, of the District of Columbia, or a person of any agency or instrumentality who is under a duty to discharge the obligation. A separate taxable entity is created if the petition is filed by an individual under Chapter 7 or Chapter 11 of the Bankruptcy Code. The tax obligations of the person filing a bankruptcy petition, the *debtor*, vary depending on the bankruptcy chapter under which the petition is filed. When a debt owed to another is canceled, the amount canceled or forgiven is considered income that is taxed to the person owing the debt. If a debt is canceled under a bankruptcy proceeding, the amount canceled is *not income*. However, the canceled debt reduces the amount of other tax benefits the debtor would otherwise be entitled to.

TAX ATTRIBUTES

Certain deduction and credit carryovers and decisions that the debtor made in earlier years are taken over by the bankruptcy estate when the petition is filed. These include carryovers of deductions, losses, and credits, the debtor's method of accounting, and the basis and holding period of assets. These are referred to as *tax attributes.*

When the estate is terminated, the debtor assumes any remaining tax attributes that were taken over by the estate as well as any attributes arising during the administration of the estate. The bankruptcy estate's income tax returns are open upon written request for inspection by the individual debtor. The disclosure is necessary so that the debtor can properly figure the amount and nature of the tax attributes, if any, that the debtor must assume when the bankruptcy estate is terminated. In addition, the debtor's income tax returns for the year the bankruptcy case begins and for earlier years are open to inspection by or disclosure to the bankruptcy estate's trustee.

TRANSFER OF ASSETS TO THE ESTATE

Bankruptcy law determines which of the debtor's assets become part of the bankruptcy estate. All of the debtor's legal and equitable interests become property of the estate, and certain property can subsequently become exempt from the estate. A transfer, other than by sale or exchange of an asset from the debtor to the bankruptcy estate, is not treated as a disposition for income tax purposes. This means that the transfer does not result in gain or loss, recapture of deductions or credits, or acceleration of income or deductions. The transfer of an installment obligation, for example, to the estate would not accelerate gain under the rules for reporting installment sales. When the bankruptcy estate is terminated, the debtor is treated the same as the estate was regarding any assets transferred back to the debtor.

The individual debtor cannot carry back any net operating loss or credit carryback from a year ending after the bankruptcy case has begun to any tax year ending before the case began. The estate, however, can carry the loss back to offset any pre-bankruptcy income.

ELECTION TO END THE TAX YEAR

If an individual debtor has assets other than those exempt from the bankruptcy estate, the debtor can choose to end his or her tax year on the day before the filing of the bankruptcy case. Then the tax year is divided into two short tax years of fewer than 12 months each. The first year ends on the day before the filing date, and the second year begins with the filing date and ends on the date the tax year normally ends. Once made, this choice cannot be changed. Any income tax liability for the first short tax year becomes an allowable claim arising before bankruptcy against the bankruptcy estate. If the tax liability is not paid in the bankruptcy proceeding, the liability is not canceled because it can be collected from the debtor as an individual. If the debtor does not choose to end the tax year, then no part of his or her tax liability for the year in which bankruptcy proceedings began can be collected from the estate.

If married, the debtor's spouse can also join in the choice to end the tax year, if the two file a joint return for the first short tax year. These choices must be made by the due date for filing the return for the first short tax year. Once the choice is made, it cannot be revoked for the first short tax year, but the choice does not mean that they must file a joint return for the second short tax year.

If the debtor's spouse files for bankruptcy later in the same year, he or she can also choose to end his or her tax year, regardless of whether he or she joined in the choice to end the debtor's tax years. Because each of the two has a separate bankruptcy, one or the other of them can have three short tax years in the same calendar year. If the debtor's spouse had joined in the choice, or if the debtor had not made the choice to end his or her tax year, the debtor can join in the spouse's choice. But if the debtor made an election and the spouse did not join in the election, the debtor cannot join in the spouse's later election. This is because the debtor and his or her spouse, having different tax years, could not file a joint return for a year ending on the date before the spouse's filing of bankruptcy.

THE BANKRUPTCY ESTATE

The filing of a bankruptcy petition for an individual debtor under Chapter 7 or Chapter 11 of the bankruptcy code created a separate taxable bankruptcy estate. The trustee for Chapter 7 cases or the debtor-in-possession for Chapter 11 cases is responsible for preparing and filing the estate's tax returns and paying its taxes. The debtor remains responsible for filing returns and paying taxes on any income that does not belong to the estate.

If a bankruptcy case begins, but later is dismissed by the bankruptcy court, the estate is not treated as a separate taxable entity. If tax returns have been filed for the estate, amended returns must be filed to move income and deductions from the estate's return to the debtor's returns.

TREATMENT OF INCOME, DEDUCTIONS, AND CREDITS

The gross income of the bankruptcy estate includes any of the debtor's gross income to which the estate is entitled under the bankruptcy law. The estate's gross income also includes any income the estate is entitled to and receives or accrues after the beginning of the bankruptcy case. Gross income of the bankruptcy estate does not include amounts received or accrued by the debtor before the bankruptcy petition date.

The bankruptcy estate can deduct or take as a credit any expenses it pays or incurs, the same way that the debtor would have deducted or credited them had he or she continued in the same trade, business, or activity and actually paid or accrued the expenses. Allowable expenses include administrative expenses, such as attorney fees and court costs.

The bankruptcy estate figures its taxable income the same way as an individual figures his or her taxable income. The estate can take one personal exemption and either individual itemized deductions, or the basic standard deduction or a married individual filing a separate return. The estate cannot take the higher standard deduction allowed for married persons filing separately who are 65 or older, or blind. The estate uses the rates for a married individual filing separately to figure the tax on its taxable income.

Bankruptcy law determines which of the debtor assets become part of the bankruptcy estate. These assets are treated the same in the estate's hands as they were in the debtor's hands. A transfer, other than by sale or exchange, of an asset from the debtor to the bankruptcy estate is not treated as a disposition for income tax purposes. This means the transfer does not result in gain or loss, recapture of deductions or credits, or acceleration of income or deductions.

When the bankruptcy estate is terminated, any resulting transfer other than by sale or exchange of the estate's assets back to the debtor is not treated as a disposition. The transfer does not result in gain or loss, recapture of deductions, or credits, or acceleration of income or deductions to the estate.

ATTRIBUTE CARRYOVERS

The bankruptcy estate must treat its tax attributes the same way that the debtor would have treated them. These items must be determined as of the first day of the debtor's tax year in which the bankruptcy case begins. The bankruptcy estate gets the following tax attributes from the debtor:

1) Net operating carryovers.
2) Carryovers of excess charitable contributions.
3) Recovery of tax benefit items.
4) Credit carryovers.
5) Capital loss carryovers.
6) Basis, holding period, and character of assets.
7) Method of accounting.
8) Passive activity loss and credit carryovers.

9)   Unused at-risk deductions.

10)   Other tax attributes as provided in regulations.

Certain tax attributes of the estate must be reduced by any excluded income from cancellation of debt occurring in a bankruptcy proceeding. If the bankruptcy estate has any tax attributes at the time it is terminated, they are assumed by the debtor.

PASSIVE AND AT-RISK ACTIVITIES

For bankruptcy cases beginning on or after November 9, 1992, passive activity carryover losses and credits and unused at-risk deductions are treated as tax attributes that the debtor passes to the bankruptcy estate and the estate passes back to the debtor when the estate terminates. Transfers to the debtor, other than by sale or exchange, of interests in passive or at-risk activities, are treated as exchanges that are not taxable. These transfers include the return of exempt property to the debtor and the abandonment of estate property to the debtor. If a bankruptcy case begins before November 9, 1992, and ends on or after that date, the debtor and the trustee for an individual Chapter 7 case and the debtor-in-possession for a Chapter 11 case can elect to have these provisions apply. In a Chapter 7 case, the election is made jointly by the debtor and the trustee of the bankruptcy estate. In a Chapter 11 case, the election is incorporated in the bankruptcy plan.

The bankruptcy estate is allowed a deduction for administrative expenses and any fees or charges assessed to it. These expenses are deductible as itemized deductions subject to the 2% floor on the miscellaneous itemized deductions. Administrative expenses attributable to the conduct of a trade or business by the bankruptcy estate or the production of the estate's rents or royalties are deductible in arriving at adjusted gross income.

The expenses are subject to disallowance under other provisions of the Internal Revenue Code, such as disallowing certain capital expenditures, taxes, or expenses relating to tax-exempt interest. These expenses can only be deducted by the estate, never by the debtor.

If the administrative expenses of the bankruptcy estate are more than its gross income for the tax year, the excess amount can be carried back three years and forward seven years. The amounts can only be carried back or forward to a tax year of the estate, never to the debtor's tax year. The excess amount to be carried back or forward is treated like a net operating loss and must first be carried back to the earliest year possible.

The bankruptcy estate can change its accounting period tax year once without getting IRS approval. This allows the trustee of the estate to close the estate tax year early, before the expected termination of the estate. The trustee can then file a return for the first short tax year to a quick determination of the estate's tax liability. If the bankruptcy estate itself has a net operating loss, separate from any losses passing to the estate from the debtor under the attribute carryover rules, the bankruptcy estate can carry the loss back not only to its own earlier tax years, but also to the debtor's tax years before the year the bankruptcy case began. The estate can also carry back excess credits, such as the business credit, to the pre-bankruptcy years.

EMPLOYER IDENTIFICATION NUMBER

The trustee or the debtor-in-possession must obtain an employer identification number (EIN) for a bankruptcy estate if the estate must file any form, statement, or document with the IRS. The trustee uses the EIN on any tax return filed for the bankruptcy estate including estimated tax returns. Trustees representing 10 or more bankruptcy estates, other than estates that will be filing employment or excise tax returns, can file a consolidated application to obtain blocks of 10 or more EINs. The Social Security number of the individual debtor cannot be used as the EIN for the bankruptcy estate.

EMPLOYMENT TAX

The trustee or debtor-in-possession must withhold income and Social Security taxes and file employment tax returns for any wages paid by the trustee or debtor, including wage claims paid as administrative expenses. Until these employment taxes are deposited as required by the IRS, they should be set apart in a separate bank account to ensure that funds are available to satisfy the liability. If the employment taxes are not paid as required, the trustee can be held personally liable for payment of the taxes.

The trustee has the duty to prepare and file *Form W-2, Wage and Tax Statement*, in connection with wage claims paid by the trustee, regardless of whether the claims accrued before or during bankruptcy. If the debtor fails to prepare and file Form W-2 for wages paid before bankruptcy, the trustee should instruct the employees to file an IRS *Form 4852, Substitute for Form W-2.*

The debtor's income tax returns for the year the bankruptcy case begins and for earlier years are, upon written request, open to inspection by or disclosure to the trustee. If the bankruptcy case was not voluntary, disclosure cannot be made before the bankruptcy court has entered an order for relief, unless the court rules the disclosure is needed for determining whether relief should be ordered.

TAX-FREE REORGANIZATIONS

The tax-free reorganization provisions of the Internal Revenue Code apply to a transfer by a corporation of all or part of its assets to another corporation in a Chapter 11 or similar case, but only if, under the reorganization plan, stock or securities of the corporation to which the assets are transferred are distributed in a transaction qualifying under the applicable section of the Code. A Chapter 11 or similar case for this purpose is a bankruptcy case under Chapter 11, or a receivership, foreclosure, or similar proceeding in a federal or state court, but only if the corporation is under the jurisdiction of the court in the case and the transfer of assets is under a plan of reorganization approved by the court. In a receivership, foreclosure, or similar proceeding before a federal or state agency involving certain financial institutions, the agency is treated as a court.

The law provides that no gain or loss is recognized if a corporation's stock is exchanged solely for stock or securities in the same or another corporation under a qualified reorganization plan. In this case the shareholders in the bankrupt corporation would recognize no gain or loss if they exchange their stock solely for stock or securities of the corporation acquiring the bankrupt's assets. The law provides that no gain or loss is recognized by a shareholder if a corporation distributes solely stock or securities of another corporation that the distributing corporation controls immediately before the distribution. In an exchange that qualifies under the legal requirements, except that other property or money besides the permitted stock or securities is received by the shareholder, gain is recognized by the shareholder only to the extent of the money and the fair market value of the other property received. No loss is recognized in this situation.

The filing of required returns becomes the responsibility of an appointed trustee, receiver, or a debtor-in-possession, rather than a corporate officer.

EXEMPTION FROM TAX RETURN FILING

If an individual is a trustee, receiver, or an assignee of a corporation that is in bankruptcy, receivership, dissolution, or in the hands of an assignee by court order, relief from filing federal income tax returns for the corporation can be obtained from the IRS District Director. A corporation that is subject to the jurisdiction of the court in a Chapter 11 or similar case is exempt from the personal holding company tax, unless the main reason for beginning or continuing the case is to avoid paying the tax.

DETERMINATION OF TAX

A bankrupt corporation, or a receiver, bankruptcy trustee, or assignee having possession of, or holding title to, substantially all the property or business of the corporation files a Form 1120 for the tax year. After the return is filed, the Internal Revenue Service can redetermine the tax liability shown on the return. When the administrative remedies with the Service have been exhausted, the tax issue, if necessary, can be litigated either in the bankruptcy court or in the U.S. Tax Court.

The trustee of the bankruptcy estate can request a determination of any unpaid liability of the estate for the taxes incurred during the administration of the case by the filing of a tax return and a request for such a determination with the IRS. Unless the return is fraudulent or contains a material misrepresentation, the trustee, the debtor, and any successor to the debtor are discharged from liability for the taxes upon payment of the taxes:

1) As determined by the IRS.

2) As determined by the bankruptcy court, after the completion of the IRS examination.

3) As shown on the return if the IRS does not notify the trustee within 60 days after the request for the determination that the return has been selected for examination.

4) As shown on the return, if the IRS does not complete the examination and notify the trustee of any tax due within 180 days after the request or any additional time permitted by the bankruptcy court.

To request a prompt determination of any unpaid tax liability of the estate, the trustee must file a written application for the determination with the IRS District Director in the district in which the bankruptcy case is pending. The application must be submitted in duplicate executed under the penalties of perjury. The trustee must submit with the application an exact copy of the return(s) filed by the trustee with the IRS for a completed tax period, and a statement of the name and location of the office where the return was filed. On the envelope must be written: *DO NOT OPEN IN MAIL ROOM.*

The IRS examination agent will notify the trustee within 60 days from receipt of the application whether the return filed by the trustee has been selected for examination or has been accepted as filed. If the return is selected for examination, it will be examined as soon as possible. The examination function will notify the trustee of any tax due within 180 days from receipt of the application, or within any additional time permitted by the bankruptcy court.

BANKRUPTCY COURT JURISDICTION

The bankruptcy court has authority to determine the amount or legality of any tax imposed on the debtor for the estate, including any fine, penalty, or addition to the tax, whether or not the tax was previously assessed or paid.

The bankruptcy court does not have authority to determine the amount or legality of a tax, fine, penalty, or addition to taxes that was contested before and finally decided by a court administrative tribunal of competent jurisdiction before the date of filing the bankruptcy petition. Also, the bankruptcy court does not have authority to decide the right of the bankruptcy estate for a tax refund until the trustee of the estate properly requests the refund from the IRS and either the Service determined the refund or 120 days pass after the date of the request.

If the debtor has already claimed a refund or credit for an overpayment of taxes on a properly filed return or claim for refund, the trustee can rely on that claim. Otherwise, if the credit or refund was not claimed by the debtor, the trustee can make the request by filing the appropriate original or amended return or form with the District Director in the district in which the bankruptcy case is pending. For overpayment of taxes of the bankruptcy estate incurred during the administration of the case, the trustee can use a properly executed tax return form as a claim for refund or credit.

The IRS examination agent, if requested by the trustee or debtor-in-possession will examine the appropriate amended return, claim, or original return filed by the trustee on an expedited basis, and will complete the examination and notify the trustee of its decision within 120 days from the date of filing of the claim.

TAX COURT JURISDICTION

The filing of a bankruptcy petition automatically results in a suspension of any U.S. Tax Court proceeding to determine the debtor's tax liability. The suspension continues until one of the acts removing it occurs. The suspension can be lifted by the bankruptcy court upon the debtor's request, the request of the IRS, or the request of any other interested party. Because the bankruptcy court has the authority to lift the suspension and allow the debtor to begin or continue a Tax Court case involving the debtor's tax liability, the bankruptcy court has, in effect, during the period of the suspension, the sole authority to determine whether the tax issue is decided in the bankruptcy court or in the Tax Court.

In any bankruptcy case, the 90-day period for filing a Tax Court petition, after the issuance of the statutory notice of deficiency, is suspension for the time the debtor is prevented from filing the petition because of the bankruptcy case, and for 60 days thereafter. Even if the statutory notice was issued before the bankruptcy petition was filed, the suspension exists if any part of the 90-day period remained at the date the bankruptcy petition was filed. The trustee of the bankruptcy estate in any Chapter 11 bankruptcy case can intervene, on behalf of the estate, in any proceeding in the U.S. Tax Court.

After the determination of a tax by either the bankruptcy court or the U.S. Tax Court, the IRS can assess the tax against the estate, or against the debtor, or the debtor's successor, subject to applicable law.

In bankruptcy situations, the IRS has limited authority to immediately assess tax deficiencies, without following the normal procedures under which it issues a deficiency notice. In a bankruptcy case, an immediate assessment of tax can be made for a tax liability incurred by the debtor's estate, or on the debtor, if the liability for the tax has been finally decided in the bankruptcy case.

No purpose would be served by requiring issuance of a deficiency notice prior to assessment of taxes imposed on the bankruptcy estate or on the debtor when the liability has been finally determined in the bankruptcy court, because in neither case can the issue be litigated in the Tax Court. In a Chapter 11 bankruptcy case, the period of limitation for assessment of taxes is three years. After the later of the date the return was due or was filed, the limitation is suspended for the period during which the IRS is prohibited, because of the bankruptcy, from making the assessment, plus 60 days thereafter.

In bankruptcy cases other than those of individuals filing under Chapter 7 or 11, and in receivership proceedings where substantially all the debtor's property is in the hands of a receiver, current and earlier returns of the debtor are upon written request, open to inspection by or disclosure to the trustee or receiver, but only if the IRS finds that the trustee or receiver has a material interest which will be affected by information on the return.

After the filing of a bankruptcy petition and during the period the debtor's assets or those of the bankruptcy estate are under the jurisdiction of the bankruptcy court, these assets are not subject to levy. The IRS can file a proof of claim in the bankruptcy court the same way as other creditors. This claim can be presented to the bankruptcy court even though the taxes have not yet been assessed or are subject to a Tax Court proceeding. In bankruptcy, the debtor's debts are assigned priorities for payment. Most of the tax debts are classified as seventh priority claims, which are certain income and other taxes that the debtor is considered to have owed before he or she files a bankruptcy petition.

The following federal taxes, if unsecured, are seventh priority taxes of the government:

1) Income taxes for tax years ending on or before the date of filing the bankruptcy petition, for which a return is due within three years of the filing.
2) Income taxes assessed within 240 days before the date of filing the petition.
3) Income taxes that were not assessed before the petition, but were assessable as of the petition.
4) Withholding taxes for which the debtor is liable in any capacity.
5) Employer's share of employment taxes on wages, salaries, or commissions, including vacation, severance, and sick leave pay which are paid as priority claims under Chapter 11.

6) Excise taxes on transactions occurring before the date of filing the bankruptcy petition for which a return is due.

7) If a return is not required, these excise taxes include only those for transactions occurring during the three years before the date of filing the petition.

Certain taxes are assigned a higher priority for payment than others. Taxes incurred during administration by the bankruptcy estate are paid first as administrative expenses. Taxes arising in the ordinary course of the debtor's business or financial affairs in an involuntary bankruptcy case, after the filing of the bankruptcy petition, but before the earlier of the appointment of a trustee or the order for relief, are included in the second priority of payment.

RELIEF FROM PENALTIES

A penalty for failure to pay taxes, including failure to pay estimated taxes, will not be imposed for any period during which a Chapter 11 bankruptcy case is pending. If the tax was incurred by the bankruptcy estate, the penalty will not be imposed if the failure to pay resulted from an order of the court finding probable insufficiency of funds of the estate to pay administrative expenses. If the tax was incurred by the debtor, the penalty will not be imposed if the tax was imposed before the earlier of the order for relief or the appointment of a trustee, and the bankruptcy petition was filed before the due date for the tax return, or the date for imposing the penalty occurs on or after the day the bankruptcy petition was filed.

The relief from the failure to pay a penalty does not apply to any penalty or order to pay or deposit tax withheld or collected from others and required to be paid over to the U.S. government; nor does it apply to any penalty for failure to file a timely return.

FUTA CREDIT

An employer is generally allowed a credit against the federal unemployment tax (FUTA) for contributions made to a state unemployment fund, if the contributions are paid by the last day for filing an unemployment tax return for the tax year. If the contributions to the state fund are paid after that date, only 90 percent of the otherwise allowable credit can be taken against the federal unemployment tax. For any unemployment tax on wages paid by the trustee of a Chapter 11 bankruptcy estate, if the failure to pay the state unemployment contributions on time was without fault by the trustee, the full amount of the credit is allowed.

STATUTE OF LIMITATIONS FOR COLLECTION

In a Chapter 11 bankruptcy case, the period of limitations for collection of taxes—10 years after assessment—is suspended for the period during which the IRS is prohibited from assessing or collecting, plus 6 months thereafter.

DISCHARGE OF UNPAID TAX

Debts are divided into two categories: dischargeable and nondischargeable. Dischargeable debts are those that the debtor is no longer personally liable to pay after the bankruptcy proceedings are concluded. Nondischargeable debts are those that are not canceled because of the bankruptcy proceedings. The debtor remains personally liable for their payment.

There is no discharge for the debtor as an individual debtor at the termination of a bankruptcy case for taxes for which no return, a late return, or a fraudulent return was filed. Claims against the debtor for other taxes predating the bankruptcy petition by more than three years can be discharged. If the IRS has a lien on the debtor property, the property can be seized to collect discharged tax debts.

If the debtor completes all payments under a Chapter 13 debt adjustment plan for an individual with regular income, the court can grant a discharge of debts, including priority debts (described above). If the debtor fails to complete all payments under the plan, the taxes are not discharged although the court can grant a discharge of other debts in limited circumstances.

If a debt is canceled or forgiven, other than as a gift or bequest, the debtor must include the canceled amount in gross income for tax purposes. A debt includes any indebtedness for which the debtor is liable or which attaches to property the debtor holds. However, a canceled debt should not be included in gross income if any of the following situations apply:

1) The cancellation takes place in a bankruptcy case under the U.S. Bankruptcy Code.
2) The cancellation takes place when the debtor is insolvent.
3) The canceled debt is qualified farm debt incurred in operating a farm.
4) The canceled debt is qualified real property business indebtedness, i.e; debt connected with business real property.

If a cancellation of debt occurs in a Chapter 11 bankruptcy case, the bankruptcy exclusion takes precedence over the insolvency, qualified farm debt, or qualified real property business indebtedness exclusions. To the extent that the taxpayer is insolvent, the insolvency exclusion takes precedence over qualified farm debt or qualified real property business indebtedness exclusions.

A bankruptcy case is a case under Chapter 11 of the U.S. Code, but only if the debtor is under the jurisdiction of the court and the cancellation of the debt is granted by the court or occurs as a result of a plan approved by the court. None of the debt canceled in a bankruptcy case is included in the debtor's gross income in the year canceled. Instead certain losses, credits, and basis of property must be reduced by the amount of excluded income, but not below zero. These losses, credits. and basis in property are called tax attributes.

A debtor is insolvent when and to the extent, his or her liabilities exceed the fair market value of the debtor's assets. The liabilities and the fair market value of assets are determined immediately before the cancellation of a debt to determine whether or not the debtor is insolvent and the amount by which he or she is insolvent. Gross income debt canceled when insolvent is excluded, but only up to the amount of the insolvency. The amount excluded must be used to reduce certain tax attributes.

REDUCTION OF TAX ATTRIBUTES

If a debtor excludes canceled debt from income because it is canceled in a bankruptcy case or during insolvency, he or she must use the excluded amount to reduce certain tax attributes. *Tax attributes* include the basis of certain assets and the losses and credits listed below. By reducing these tax attributes, tax on the canceled debt is in part postponed instead of being entirely forgiven. This prevents an excessive tax benefit from the debt cancellation.

If a separate bankruptcy estate was created, the trustee or debtor-in-possession must reduce the estate's attributes, but not below zero, by the canceled debt.

The amount of canceled debt is used to reduce the tax attributes in the order listed below. However, the debtor can choose to use all or a part of the amount of canceled debt to first reduce the basis of depreciable property before reducing the other tax attributes.

Net operating loss. Reduction of tax attributes is in the following order:

1) Any net operating loss for the tax year in which the debt cancellation takes place.

2) Any net operating loss carryover to that tax year.

General business credit carryovers. Any carryovers, to or from the tax year of the debt cancellation, of amounts used to determine the general business credit are reduced.

Minimum tax credit. Any minimum tax credit that is available at the beginning of the tax year following the tax year of the debt cancellation is reduced. This only applies to debt canceled in tax years beginning after 1993.

Capital Losses. Any net capital loss for the tax year of the debt cancellation, and any capital loss carryover to that year are reduced.

Basis. The basis (see Basis Reduction below) of the debtor's property is reduced. This reduction applies to the basis of both depreciable and nondepreciable property.

Passive Activity Loss and Credit Carryovers. Reduce any passive activity loss or credit carryover from the tax year of the debt cancellation. This applies to debt canceled in tax years beginning after 1993.

Foreign Tax Credit. Any carryover, to or from the tax year of the debt cancellation, of an amount used to determine the foreign tax credit or the Puerto Rico and other possessions' tax credits is reduced.

Except for the credit carryovers, the tax attributes are reduced one dollar for each one dollar of canceled debt that is excluded from income. The credit carryovers are reduced by 33-1/2 cents for each dollar of canceled debt that is excluded from income. The required reductions in tax attributes are to be made after figuring the tax for the year of the debt cancellation. In reducing net operating losses and capital losses, the loss for the tax year of the debt cancellation is reduced first, and then any loss carryover to that year in the order in which the carryovers are taken into account for the tax year of the debt cancellation.

In an individual bankruptcy under Chapter 7 (liquidation) or Chapter 11 (reorganization) of Chapter 11 of the U.S. Code, the required reduction of tax attributes must be made to the attributes of the bankruptcy estate, a separate taxable entity resulting from the filing of the case. Also, the trustee of the bankruptcy estate must make the choice of whether to reduce the basis of depreciable property first before reducing other tax attributes.

BASIS REDUCTION

If any amount of the debt cancellation is used to reduce the basis of assets, the following rules apply to the extent indicated.

When to make the basis reduction. The reduction in basis is to be made at the beginning of the tax years following the tax year of the debt cancellation. The reduction applies to property held at that time.

Bankruptcy and insolvency reduction limit. The reduction in basis because of canceled debt in bankruptcy or in insolvency cannot be more than the total basis of property held immediately after the debt cancellation, minus the total liabilities immediately after the cancellation. This limit does not apply if an election is made to reduce basis before reducing other attributes.

Exempt property under Chapter 11. If debt is canceled in a bankruptcy case under Chapter 11, no reduction is made in basis for property that the debtor treats as exempt property.

Election to reduce basis first. In the event of an individual bankruptcy case under Chapter 7 or 11, the estate can choose to reduce the basis or depreciable property before reducing any other tax attributes. This reduction of the basis of depreciable property cannot be more than the total basis of depreciable property held at the beginning of the tax year following the tax year of the debt cancellation.

Depreciable property means any property subject to depreciation, but only if a reduction of the basis will reduce the amount of depreciation or amortization otherwise allowable for the period immediately following the basis reduction. The debtor may choose to treat as depreciable property any real property that is stock in trade or is held primarily for sale to customers in the ordinary course of trade or business. The debtor must make this choice on the tax return for the tax year of the debt cancellation, and once made, he or she can revoke it only with IRS approval. If the debtor establishes reasonable cause, he or she can make the choice with an amended return or claim for refund or credit.

An election should be made to reduce the basis of depreciable property before reducing other tax attributes as well as the election to treat real property inventory as appreciable property. If any basis in property is reduced and is later sold or otherwise disposed of again, the part of the gain that is attributable to this basis reduction is taxable as ordinary income. The ordinary income part can be figured by treating the amount of the basis reduction as a depreciation deduction. A determination is made of what would have been straight line depreciation as though there had been no basis reduction for debt cancellation.

PARTNERSHIPS

If a partnership's debt is canceled because of bankruptcy or insolvency, the rules for the exclusion of the canceled amount from gross income and for tax attribute reduction are applied at the individual partner level. Each partner's share of the debt cancellation income must be reported on the partners return unless the partner meets the bankruptcy or insolvency exclusion. Then all choices, such as the choices to reduce the basis of depreciable property before reducing other tax attributes, to treat real property inventory as depreciable property, and to end the tax year on the day before filing the bankruptcy case, must be made by the individual partners, not the partnership.

For purposes of reducing the basis of depreciable property in attribute reduction, a partner treats his or her partnership interest as depreciable property to the extent of the partner's proportionate interest in the partnership's depreciable property. This applies only if the partnership makes a corresponding reduction in the partnership's basis in its depreciable property with respect to the partner. The allocation of an amount of debt cancellation income to a partner results in the partner's basis on the partnership being increased by that amount. At the same time, the reduction in the partner's share of partnership liabilities caused by the debt cancellation results in a reduction of the partner's basis in the partnership. These basis adjustments are separate from any basis reduction under the attribute reduction rules.

CORPORATIONS

In a bankruptcy proceeding or insolvency, corporations follow the same rules for debt cancellation and reduction of tax attributes as an individual or individual bankruptcy estate would follow. A different rule might exist when a corporation's stock is transferred in exchange for its own debt. This stock for debt exception is repealed for transfers made after 1994 unless the corporation filed for bankruptcy for a similar court proceeding before 1994. The principal difference between the stock for debt exception and the general treatment is that the corporation does not reduce its tax attributes under the stock for debt exception.

STOCK FOR DEBT RULES

If a corporation transfers its stock in satisfaction of indebtedness and the fair market value of its stock is less than the indebtedness it owes, the corporation has income to the extent of the difference from the cancellation of indebtedness. After 1994, a corporation can exclude all or a portion of the income created by the stock for debt transfer if it is in a bankruptcy proceeding or, if not in a bankruptcy proceeding, it can exclude the income to the extent it is insolvent. The corporation must reduce its tax attributes to the extent it has any by the amount of excluded income. Before 1995, a corporation did not realize income because of such stock for debt exchanges if it was in bankruptcy or to the extent it was insolvent. Consequently, there is no gross income to exclude, and no reduction of its tax attributes is necessary. This provision applies only to stock transferred before 1995 in satisfaction of its debt, unless the bankruptcy or a similar court procedure was filed before 1994.

The stock for debt exception does not apply if:

1) The corporation issues nominal or token shares.
2) The value of stock received by the creditor in exchange for cancellation of the debt is less than half the value of the stock that the creditor would receive if all the corporation's unsecured creditors taking part in the workout received a pro rata amount of stock issued.

A corporation that is in bankruptcy or to the extent that it is insolvent can exclude the debt cancellation income, but it must reduce its tax attributes—to the extent it has any. (See Tax Attributes, above.) A *workout* includes a Chapter 11 bankruptcy case or other transaction or series of transactions involving a significant restructuring of the debt of a corporation in financial difficulty.

S Corporations

For S corporations, the rules for excluding income from debt cancellation because of bankruptcy or insolvency apply at the corporate level. A loss or deduction that is disallowed for the tax year of the debt cancellation, because it exceeds the shareholders' basis in the corporation's stock and debt, is treated as a net operating loss for that tax year in making the required deduction of tax attributes for the amount of the canceled debt.

Chapter 7

Using a Home for Business Purposes

DEFINING A HOME

For purposes of this discussion, the term *home* includes a house, apartment, condominium, mobile home, boat, and structures on the property. Included are unattached garages, studios, barns, or greenhouses. The term does not include any part of a taxpayer's property which is used exclusively as a hotel or inn.

Whether a taxpayer is an employee or self-employed, expenses cannot be deducted for the business use of the taxpayer's home. A limited deduction for a home or business use can be taken if the home is used exclusively and regularly:

1) As the principal place of business for any trade or business in which the taxpayer is engaged.
2) As a place to deal with patients, clients, or customers, in the normal course of a trade or business.
3) If there is a separate structure for a trade or business that is not attached to the taxpayer's home.

However, regardless of whether the exclusive and regular use tests are met, a deduction cannot be taken for the business use of a home if the taxpayer is an employee and either of the following situations applies:

1) The business use of the home is not for the convenience of the taxpayer's employer. Whether a home's business use is for the employer's convenience depends on all the facts and circumstances. However, business

use is not considered for an employer's convenience merely because it is appropriate and helpful to use the home for business purposes.

2) The taxpayer rents all of his or her home to the employer and uses the rented portion to perform services as an employee.

The home must be used in connection with a trade or business to take a deduction for its business use. If the home is used for a profit-seeking activity that is not a trade or business, no deduction can be taken for its business use.

EXCLUSIVE USE

Exclusive use means only for business. If the home is used in part for the taxpayer's business and part for personal purposes, a business deduction cannot be claimed for using it. There are two exceptions to the exclusive use rule:

1) The use of part of the home for storage of inventory.
2) The use of part of the home as a day-care facility.

The storage of inventory exception must meet all of the following five requirements:

1) The inventory must be for use by the taxpayer's trade or business.
2) The trade or business must be the wholesale or retail selling of products.
3) The home that is used must be the only fixed location of the trade or business.
4) The storage space must be used on a regular basis.
5) The space used must be a separately identifiable space suitable for storage.

Regular use means on a continuing basis. Occasional or incidental business use of part of a home does not meet the regular use requirements, even if that part is used for no other purpose.

It is permissible to have more than one business location, including a home, for a single trade or business. To deduct expenses for business use of a home, it must be the principal place of business for the trade or business based on all the facts and circumstances. The two primary factors are:

1) The relative importance of the activities performed at each business location.
2) The amount of time spent at each location.

A comparison of the relative importance of the activities performed at each business location depends on the characteristics of each business. If the nature of a business requires that the taxpayer meet or confer with clients or patients, or requires that goods or services are delivered to a customer, the place where that contact occurs must be given weight in determining where the most important activities are performed. Performance of necessary or essential activities in a home office, such as billing or accounting for goods or service, are not necessarily controlling.

If the relative importance cannot be clearly established for a home as the principal place of business, then the time spent in the home conducting business is the significant consideration. A comparison must be made with the amount of time spent on business in a home office with the amount of time spent at other locations. It is possible that there is no principal place of business. Whether a home office is the principal place of business must be determined separately for each trade or business activity. One home office can be the principal place of business for more than one activity; the exclusive use test for any activity will not be met unless each activity conducted in that office meets all the requirement for the business use of the home deduction.

When patients, clients, or customers are met and dealt with in a home in the normal course of the business, and even though the business is carried on at another location, expenses can be deducted for the part of the home used exclusively and regularly for business. The use of a home must be substantial and necessary for the conduct of the business; occasional meetings and telephone calls do not qualify for a deduction of expenses for a business use of a home.

Partial Deductions

If part of a home is used for business and meets the necessary requirements for deductions, the expenses must be divided between operating the home for business use and personal use. Some expenses paid to maintain the home are directly related to its business use; some are indirectly related and some are unrelated. All direct expenses and part of any indirect expenses can be deducted. If the cash method of accounting is used, the only expenses that can be deducted are those paid during the tax year. The cash method can be used to deduct expenses when they are actually paid. The total expenses deducted for business use of a home are limited to the gross income from the business use of a home. A deduction for business cannot be taken for expenses incurred during any part of the year that a home was not used for business purposes.

Types of Expenses

Direct expenses benefit only the business part of home use. They can include painting or repairs made in the specific area or room used for business. Direct expenses for a portion of a home used regularly, but not exclusively, as a day-care facility must be adjusted for the time the space is used for business. Indirect expenses are for keeping up and running the entire home. They benefit both the business and personal parts of the home. Examples of indirect expenses include real estate taxes, mortgage interest deduction, casualty losses, rent, utilities and services, insurance, repairs, security systems, and depreciation. The percentage of indirect expense used for business can be deducted. The business percentage is calculated by dividing the area used for business by the total area of the home including the basement. The area is measured in square feet. To figure the percentage of the home used for business, divide the number of square feet of space used for business by the total number of square feet of space in the home. The business percentage can also be determined by dividing the number of rooms used for business by the number of rooms in the home. It is allowable to use any other reasonable method of calculation to determine the business percentage.

(The following are excerpts of several deductions that can be made to calculate the business deduction of various expenses.)

To figure the business part of real estate taxes, multiply the real estate taxes paid by the percentage of the home used for business. For deductible mortgage interest, multiply the total interest by the percentage of the home used in business. Interest on a second mortgage can be included in this computation. If a casualty loss is sustained, the business part of the loss can be deducted as a business expense. A casualty loss is treated as an *unrelated expense,* a *direct expense,* or an *indirect expense,* depending on the property affected.

1) If the loss is on property used only in the business, the entire loss is a business deduction—a direct expense.

2) If the loss is on a portion of the home or other property that is not used specifically in the business, no business deduction is allowed—an unrelated expense.

3) If the loss is on property that can be used for both business and personal purposes, only the business part is a business deduction—an indirect expense.

If the home or other business property is completely destroyed, i.e; becomes totally worthless, the deductible loss is the adjusted basis of the property, minus any salvage value and any insurance or other reimbursement that is received or expected to be received. The loss is figured without taking into account any decrease in fair market value. If the business property is stolen from the home, the deductible loss is the adjusted basis in the property, reduced by any insurance or other reimbursement received or expected to be received. In a partial destruction of business (or nonbusiness) use property, the deductible loss is the decrease in fair market value of the property or the adjusted basis of the property, whichever is less. This amount must be reduced by any insurance or other reimbursement that is received or expected to be received.

Casualty losses to nonbusiness use property are only deductible if deductions are itemized and the loss exceeds $100 and all casualty losses exceed 10%of the taxpayer's adjusted gross income. For a loss on property which is used both for business and nonbusiness purposes, these limits will apply only to the nonbusiness part.

If a home is rented rather than owned, and the home meets the requirements for business use, part of the rent paid can be deducted. The rent payments are multiplied by the percentage of the home used for business. Expenses for utilities and services are primarily personal expenses. However, if part of the home is used for business, the business portion of those expenses can be deducted. The business percentage is calculated for utilities using the same method as the percentage of the home used for business was calculated. The cost of repairs and supplies that relate to the business, including labor other than the owner's labor, is a deductible expense. Repairs keep the home in good working order over its useful life.

The cost of insurance that covers the business part of the home is deductible. If the insurance premium covers the property for a period that extends past the end of the individual's tax year, only the business percentage of the part of the premium that covers for the taxpayer's tax year is deductible. The remaining part of the current tax year is applied to the following year tax.

If a security system is installed that protects all the doors and windows in the home, the business part of the security premium expense can be deducted. A depreciation deduction can be taken for the part of the cost of the security system relating to the business percentage-use of the home. The cost of property that will be used for more than one year, such as a building, a permanent improvement, or furniture, is a capital expenditure; the costs cannot be deducted in one year. The cost can be recovered by taking annual deductions for depreciation. Land is not depreciable property, so the cost of land cannot be recovered until the property is sold.

A permanent improvement increases the value of property, adds to its life, and gives it a possible different use. If the repairs are part of an extensive remodeling or restoration of the home, the entire job is an improvement and a distinction must be made between repairs and improvements. Accurate records of the expenditures must be kept which will help the user to decide whether an expenditure is a deductible expense or a capital expenditure.

DEPRECIATION

The basis of the property must be decreased by the amount of depreciation that has been deducted using the method of depreciation that was chosen. If less depreciation was taken than could have been, the basis still must be decreased by the amount that could have been taken. If more depreciation has been taken than should have been, the basis must be decreased by the amount that should have been deducted plus the part of the excess deducted that actually decreased the tax liability for any year. To figure the depreciation on the business part of a home, the taxpayer must know:

1) The business-use percentage of the home.
2) The first month in the tax year for which the business use of the home started.
3) The adjusted basis and fair market value of the home at the time it is to be qualified for a deduction.

If ACRS or MACRS, or some other accelerated method is used to figure depreciation on a home, some of the gain on the sale of the business part of the home can be treated as ordinary income.

If the gross income of the taxpayer from the business use of a home equals or exceeds the total business expenses, including depreciation, all of the business expenses for the use of the home can be deducted. If the gross income from the use of the home is less than the total business expenses, the deduction for certain expenses for the business use of a home is limited. The total of the deductions for otherwise nondeductible expenses, such as utilities, insurance, and depreciation cannot be more than the taxpayer's gross from the business use of the home minus the *sum* of:

1) The business percentage of the otherwise deductible mortgage interest, real taxes, and casualty and theft losses.
2) The business expenses that are not attributable to the business use of the home.

CARRYFORWARDS

Deductions over the current year's limit can be carried forward to the next tax year. These deductions are subject to the gross income limit from the business use of the home for the next tax year. The amount carried forward is allowable only up to the taxpayer's gross income in the next tax year from the business in which the deduction arose, whether or not the taxpayer lived in the home during that year.

If an employee, the use of home deductions must be itemized on Form 1040 to claim expenses for the business use of a home and other employee business expenses. Schedule A is used to claim expenses for the business use of the employee's home and any other employee business expenses. If a person is a statutory employee, Schedule C, Form 1040, is used to claim the expenses. The employee accounts to his or her employer when the employer is given documentary evidence and an account book, diary, or similar statement to verify the amount, time, place, and business purpose of each expense. An employee is treated as accounting to his or her employer if the employer gives the employee a fixed allowance under an accountable plan that is similar in form to an allowance specified by the federal government and the time, place, and business purpose of the expense is verified.

DAYCARE EXPENSES

Daycare expenses for using part of a home for daycare are deductible, if the home is used on a *regular basis* and the following requirements are met:

1) The owner of the home must be in the trade or business of providing day care for children, for persons 65 or older, or for persons who are physically or mentally unable to care for themselves.

2) The homeowner must have applied for, been granted, or be exempt from having a license, certification, registration, or approval as a day-care center, or as a family or group day-care home under applicable state law. This requirement is not met if an application was rejected, or a person's license or other authorization has been revoked.

If a part of a home is regularly used for daycare, the percentage is figured for the part of the home that is used exclusively for day care, and all that percentage of all of the allocable expenses can be deducted, subject to the deduction limits. A room that is available for use throughout each business day and regularly used in the business is considered to be used for daycare throughout each business day. Records do not have to be kept to show the specific hours the area was used for business; the area may occasionally be used for personal reasons, but a room used only occasionally for business purposes does not qualify for expense deductions.

WHAT HAPPENS WHEN A HOME IS SOLD?

If the taxpayer's home is sold, and another that costs more than the sale price of the old home is bought within two years, any gain on the sale can be postponed; but, if in the year of sale business expenses were deducted for business use of a part of the home, recognizing gain can be postponed only on the non-business part. Any gain on the business part must be recognized. If the home is sold at a loss, the loss can be deducted on the nonbusiness part.

Chapter 8

An Employer's Tax Guide Update

With the June 1995 White House Small Business Conference having cited the classification of workers as their most pressing tax concern, two bills to clarify the definition of an independent contractor having been introduced in Congress, and the IRS feeling pressure to increase compliance to existing laws, Small Business enterprises and their CPAs should be very circumspect about classification of independent contractors and employees. It is imperative that they be thoroughly aware of the worker classification differences and the respective tax-related liabilities.

WHO ARE EMPLOYEES?

Independent Contractors. Persons such as lawyers, contractors, subcontractors, public stenographers, and auctioneers, who follow an independent trade, business, or profession in which they offer their services to the public, are generally not employees. However, whether such people are employees or independent contractors depends on the facts in each case.

The general rule is that an individual is an independent contractor if he or she, the payer, has the right to control or direct only the result of the work and not the means and methods of accomplishing the result.

Common-Law Employees. Under common-law rules, every individual who performs services under the will and control of a payer, as to both what must be done and how it must be done, is an employee. It does not matter that the employer allows the employee discretion and freedom of action, as long as the employer has the legal right to control both the method and the result of the services.

Statutory Employees. Only workers in the following four categories are called statutory employees:

1) A driver who distributes beverages (other than milk), meat, vegetables, fruit, or bakery products, or who picks up and delivers laundry or dry cleaning, if the driver is paid on commission or is a company agent.

2) A full-time life insurance sales agent whose principal business activity is selling life insurance or annuity contracts, or both, primarily for one life insurance company.

3) An individual who works at home on materials or goods that a company supplies and that must be returned to the company or to a person named.

4) A full-time traveling or city salesperson who works on behalf of a company and turns in orders to the company from wholesalers, retailers, contractors, or operators of hotels, restaurants, or other establishments.

The goods sold must be merchandise for resale or supplies for use in the buyer's business operation. The work performed for the company must be the salesperson's principal business activity.

Social Security and Medicare taxes should be withheld if all three of the following conditions apply:

1) The service contract states or implies that almost all of the services are to be performed personally by them.

2) They have little or no investment in the equipment and property used to perform the services, other than an investment in transportation facilities.

3) The services are performed on a continuing basis for the same payer. Income taxes are not withheld from statutory employees.

There are two categories of statutory nonemployees—direct sellers and licensed real estate agents. They are treated as self-employed for federal income taxes and employment tax purposes if:

1) Subsequently all payments for their services as direct sellers or real estate agents are directly related to sales or other output, rather than to the number of hours worked.

2) Their services are performed under a written contract providing that they will not be treated as employees for federal tax purposes.

Direct sellers are persons engaged in selling or soliciting the sale of consumer products:

1) In the home or at a place of business other than in a permanent retail establishment.

2) To any buyer on a buy-sell basis, a deposit-commission basis, or any similar basis prescribed by regulation, for resale in the home or at a place of business other than in a permanent retail establishment.

Direct selling includes activities of individuals who attempt to increase direct sales activities of their direct sellers and who earn income based on the productivity of their direct sellers. Such activities include providing motivation and encouragement, imparting skills, knowledge, or experience, and recruiting.

Licensed real estate agents include individuals engaged in appraisal activities for real estate sales, if they earn income based on sales or other output.

MISCLASSIFICATION OF EMPLOYEES

If an employee is classified as an independent contractor and the employer had no reasonable basis for doing so, the employer can be held liable for employment taxes for that worker. If the employer does not withhold income, social security, and Medicare taxes from the employee's wages, the employer can be held personally liable for a penalty equal to the taxes that should have been paid.

If an employer has a reasonable basis for not treating a worker as an employee, the employer may be relieved from having to pay employment taxes for that worker. To get this relief, the employer must file all required federal tax returns, including information returns, on a basis consistent with the treatment of the worker. This relief provision does not apply to a worker who provides services to another business, the client, as a technical specialist under an arrangement between the business providing the worker, such as a technical services firm, and the client.

A *technical service specialist* is an engineer, designer, drafter, computer programmer, system analyst, or other similarly skilled worker engaged in a similar line of work. This rule does not automatically convert technical services specialists to employees for employment tax purposes. The common-law standards control whether the specialist is treated as an employee or an independent contractor. However, if an employer directly contracts with a technical service specialist to provide services for the employer's business rather than for another business, the employer may still be entitled to the relief provision.

Employee or Independent Contractor?

An employer must generally withhold income taxes, withhold and pay Social Security and Medicare taxes, and pay unemployment taxes on wages paid to an employee. An employer does not have to withhold or pay any taxes on payments to independent contractors. To help an employer determine whether an individual is an employee, the IRS has developed 20 factors that should be used as guidelines to determine whether sufficient control is present to establish an employer-employee relationship. Not every factor is applicable in every situation, and the degree of importance of each factor varies depending on the type of work and individual circumstances. All relevant factors, however, are considered in making a determination, and no one factor is decisive.

It does not matter that a written agreement may take a position with regard to any factors or state that certain factors do not apply if the facts indicate otherwise. If an employer treats an employee as an independent contractor and the relief provisions discussed earlier do not apply, the person responsible for the collection and payment of withholding taxes may be held personally liable for an amount equal to the taxes that should have been withheld.

The 20 factors indicating whether an individual is an employee or an independent contractor follow:

1) *Instructions.* An employee must comply with instructions about when, where, and how to work. Even if no instructions are given, the control factor is present if the employer has the right to control how the work results are achieved.

2) *Training.* An employee may be trained to perform services in a particular manner. Independent contractors ordinarily use their own methods and receive no training from the purchasers of their services.

3) *Integration.* An employee's services are usually integrated into the business operations because the services are important to the success or continuation of the business. This shows that the employee is subject to direction and control.

4) *Services Are Rendered Personally.* An employee renders services personally. This shows that the employer is interested in the methods as well as the results.

5) *Hiring Assistants.* An employee works for an employer who hires, supervises, and pays workers. An independent contractor can hire, supervise, and pay assistants under a contract that requires their contractor to provide materials and labor and to be responsible only for the result.

6) *Continuing Relationship.* An employee generally has a continuing relationship that may exist even if work is performed at recurring although irregular intervals.

7) *Set Hours of Work.* An employee usually has set hours of work established by an employer. Independent contractors generally can set their own work hours.

8) *Full-Time Required.* An employee may be required to work or be available full-time. This indicates control by the employer. An independent contractor can work when and for whom he or she chooses.

9) *Work Done on Premises.* An employee usually works on the premises of an employer, or works on a route or at a location designated by an employer.

10) *Order or Sequence Set.* An employee may be required to perform services in the order or sequence set by an employer. This shows that the employee is subject to direction and control.

11) *Reports.* An employee may be required to submit reports to an employer, which shows that the employer maintains a degree of control.

12) *Payments.* An employee generally is paid by the hour, week, or month. An independent contractor is usually paid by the job or on a straight commission.

13) *Expenses.* An employee's business and travel expenses are generally paid by an employer. This shows that the employee is subject to regulation and control.

14) *Tools and Materials.* An employee is normally furnished significant tools, materials, and other equipment by an employer.

15) *Investment.* An independent contractor has a significant investment in the facilities used in performing services for someone else.

16) *Profit or Loss.* An independent contractor can make a profit or suffer a loss.

17) *Works for More than One Person or Firm.* An independent contractor is generally free to provide services to two or more unrelated persons or firms at the same time.

18) *Offers Services to General Public.* An independent contractor makes services available to the general public.

19) *Right to Fire.* An employee can be fired by an employer. An independent contractor cannot be fired as long as results are produced that meet the specifications of the contract.

20) *Right to Quit.* An employee can quit a job at any time without incurring liability. An independent contractor usually agrees to complete a specific job and is responsible for its satisfactory completion, or legally is obligated to make good for failure to complete it.

In doubtful cases, the facts will determine whether or not there is an actual employer-employee relationship. If the taxpayer wants the IRS to determine whether a worker is an employee, *Form SS-8, Determination of Employee Work Status for Purposes of Federal Employment Taxes*, is filed with the District Director.

EMPLOYEES OF EXEMPT ORGANIZATIONS

Many nonprofit organizations are exempt from income taxes. Although they do not have to pay income taxes themselves, they must still withhold income taxes from the pay of their employees. There are special Social Security, Medicare, and federal unemployment tax rules that apply to the wages paid to the organization's employees. Nonprofit organizations include any community chest fund, or foundation, organized and operated exclusively for religious, charitable, scientific, testing for public safety, literary, or educational purposes, or to foster national or international amateur sports competition, or for the prevention of cruelty to children or animals. These organizations are usually corporations and are exempt from income taxes. Wages paid to employees of nonprofit organizations are subject to Social Security and Medicare taxes unless one of the following situations applies:

1) The organization pays an employee less than $100 in a calendar year.

2) The organization is wholly owned by a state or its political subdivision. Such an organization should contact the appropriate state official for information about reporting and getting Social Security and Medicare coverage for its employees.

3) The organization is a church or church-controlled organization opposed to the payment of Social Security and Medicare taxes for religious reasons and has filed *Form 8274, Certification for Exemption from Social Security and Medicare Taxes*. The organization must have filed for exemption before the first date on which a quarterly employment tax return would otherwise be due.

An employee of a church or church-controlled organization that is exempt from Social Security and Medicare taxes must pay self-employment taxes if the employee is paid $108.28, or more, in a year. An employee who is a member of a qualified religious sect can apply for an exemption from the self-employment tax by filing *Form 4029, Application for Exemption from Social Security and Medicare Taxes and Waiver of Benefits*. An organization that is exempt from income taxes is also exempt from the federal unemployment tax. This exemption cannot be waived.

MINISTERS

Ministers are individuals who are duly *ordained*, *commissioned*, or *licensed* by a religious body constituting a church or church denomination. They are given the authority to conduct religious worship, reform sacerdotal functions, and administer ordinances and sacraments according to the prescribed tenets and practices of that religious organization.

A minister who performs services according to an organization's will and control is its employee. The common-law rules should be applied to determine whether a minister is an employee or is self-employed. The earnings of a minister are not subject to Social Security and Medicare tax withholding. They are subject to self-employment taxes, which are not withheld from wages earned by a minister. An employer may agree with a minister to voluntarily withhold taxes to cover the minister's liability for the self-employment and income taxes.

If an employee is an ordained minister, the employer reports all taxable compensation as wages on Form W-2. Included in this amount are expense allowances or reimbursements paid under a nonaccountable plan. A parsonage allowance (housing allowance) is not included in this amount; a parsonage allowance may be reported, including any allowances for utilities and the rental value of housing provided, in a separate statement or as "Other" on the W-2, no amount shown as Social Security or Medicare; if taxes are withheld from the minister under a voluntary agreement, the amount should be shown as income tax withheld.

EMPLOYEE ACHIEVEMENT AWARDS

Taxes are not withheld on income, Social Security, or Medicare taxes on the fair market value of an employee achievement award if it is excludable from the employee's gross income. To be excludable from an employee's gross income, the award must be tangible personal property—not cash or securities—given to an employee for length of service or safety achievement, awarded as part of a meaningful presentation, and awarded under circumstances that do not indicate that the payment is disguised compensation. Excludable employee achievement awards are not subject to federal unemployment taxes.

The most that can be excluded for the cost of all employee achievement awards to the same employee for the year is $400. A higher limit of $1,600 applies to qualified plan awards. These awards are employee achievement awards under a written plan that does not discriminate in favor of highly compensated employees. An award cannot be treated as a qualified plan award if the average cost per recipient of all awards under a qualified plan is more than $400. If, during the year, an employee receives awards not made under a qualified plan and also receives awards under a qualified plan, the exclusion for the total cost of all awards to that employee cannot be more than $1,600. The $400 and $1,600 limits cannot be added together to exclude more than $1,600 for the cost of awards to any one employee during the year.

SCHOLARSHIP AND FELLOWSHIP PAYMENTS

Only amounts paid to a qualified scholarship to a candidate for a degree may be excluded from the recipient's gross income. A qualified scholarship is any amount granted as a scholarship or fellowship that is used for:

1) Tuition and fees required to enroll in, or to attend, an educational institution.
2) Fees, books, supplies, and equipment that are required for courses at the educational institution.

Any amounts paid by an employer for employees' room and board, and any amounts paid for teaching, research, or other services required as a condition of receiving the scholarship, are not excludable from the recipient's gross income. A qualified scholarship is not subject to Social Security, Medicare, and federal unemployment taxes, or income tax withholding.

DEPENDENT CARE ASSISTANCE PROGRAMS

The maximum amount that can be excluded from an employee's gross income for dependent care assistance is $5,000; $2,500 each for married taxpayers filing separate returns. The excluded amount is not subject to Social Security, Medicare, and federal unemployment taxes, or income tax withholding. If the dependent is cared for in a facility at the employer's place of business, the amount to exclude from the employee's income is based on his or her use of the facility and value of the services provided.

If an employer is the provider of dependent care, or pays a provider of dependent care directly, the employee may ask the employer for help in completing a *Form W-10, Dependent Care Provider's Identification and Certification*. The dependent care credit and the exclusion for employer-provided dependent care assistance benefits cannot be claimed by an employee unless the recipient of dependent care provided is identified by name, address, and taxpayer identification number. The dependent care provider is required to furnish this information on the Form W-10.

BACKUP

Backup is treated as wages and withheld, and employment taxes are paid as appropriate. If back pay was awarded by a court or government agency to enforce a federal or state statute protecting an employee's right to employment or wages, special rules apply for reporting those wages to the Social Security Administration. These rules also apply to litigation actions, and settlement agreements or agency directives that are resolved out of court and not under a court decree or order.

SUPPLEMENTAL UNEMPLOYMENT BENEFITS

If an employer pays, under a plan, supplemental unemployment to a former employee, all or part of the payments may be taxable, depending on how the plan is funded. Amounts that represent a return to the employee of amounts previously subject to taxes are not taxable and are not subject to withholding. The employer should withhold income taxes on the taxable part of the payments made, under a plan, to an employee who is involuntarily separated because of a reduction in force, discontinuance of a plant or operation, or other similar condition. It does not matter whether the separation is temporary or permanent. Withholding on taxable supplemental unemployment benefits must be based on the withholding certificate, Form W-4, that the employee gave to his or her employer.

INTEREST-FREE AND BELOW-MARKET-INTEREST-RATE LOANS

If an employer lends an employee more than $1,000 at less than the applicable federal interest rate, the employer is considered to have paid additional compensation to the employee to the difference between the applicable federal interest rate and the interest rate charged. This rule applies to any such loan, regardless of amount, if one of its principal purposes is the avoidance of federal taxes. The additional compensation to the employee is subject to Social Security, Medicare, and federal unemployment taxes (FUTA) but not to income tax withholding.

GROUP-TERM LIFE INSURANCE

The cost of group-term life insurance provided to an employee by the employer should be included in taxable income and wages for Social Security and Medicare tax purposes, also the cost of group-term life insurance provided to an employee for coverage over $50,000, or for coverage that discriminated in favor of an employee. This amount is subject to withholding for Social Security and Medicare taxes, but not income tax. The taxable insurance cost is treated as paid at least once a year. For coverage of taxable group-life insurance provided to former employees, including retirees, the former employees must pay the employee's share of Social Security and Medicare taxes with their income tax returns. The employer must separately include on the Form W-2 the portion of wages that consists of payments for group-term life insurance and the amount of Social Security and Medicare taxes owed by the former employee for coverage provided after separation from service.

CAFETERIA PLANS

Cafeteria plans, including flexible spending arrangements, are benefit plans under which all participants are employees who can choose from among cash and certain qualified benefits. If the employee elects qualified benefits, employer contributions are excluded from the employee's wages if the benefits are excludable from gross income under a specific section of the Internal Revenue Code, other than for scholarship and fellowship grants, and for employee fringe benefits. The cost of group-term life insurance that is includable in income only because the insurance exceeds $50,000 of coverage or is on the life of the employee's spouse or children is considered a qualified benefit under a special rule. Qualified benefits under a cafeteria plan are not subject to Social Security, Medicare, and federal unemployment taxes, or income tax withholding. If an employee chooses to receive cash instead of any qualified benefit, it is treated as wages subject to all employment taxes.

EMPLOYEE STOCK OPTIONS

There are two classes of stock options—statutory, which is covered by specific Code provisions, and nonstatutory. Statutory stock options are not taxable to the employee either when the option is granted or when it is exercised, unless the stock is disposed of in a disqualifying disposition. Nonstatutory stock options are taxable to the employee as wages when the option is exercised. These wages are subject to Social Security and Medicare taxes, income tax withholding, and federal unemployment taxes.

CONTRIBUTIONS TO A SIMPLIFIED EMPLOYEE PENSION (SEP) PLAN

An employer's SEP contributions to an employee's individual retirement arrangement (IRA) are excluded from the employee's gross income. These excluded amounts are subject to Social Security, Medicare, and federal unemployment taxes, or income tax withholding. Any employer SEP contributions paid under a salary reduction agreement are included in wages for purposes of Social Security and Medicare taxes and the federal unemployment tax.

EMPLOYEE FRINGE BENEFITS

Fringe benefits provided by an employer are excluded from the employee's gross income. The benefits are not subject to Social Security, Medicare, and federal unemployment taxes, or income tax withholding. Examples of these fringe benefits follow.

A *no-additional cost service*, which is a service offer for sale to customers in the course of the employer's line of business in which the employee works. It is provided at no substantial additional cost, including lost revenue, to the employer. Examples include airline, bus, and train tickets and telephone services provided free or at reduced rates by an employer in the line of business in which the employee works.

A *qualified employee discount* that, if offered for property, is not more than the employer's gross profit percentage. If offered for services, the discount is not more than 20 percent of the price for services offered to customers.

A *working condition benefit* that is property or a service the employee could deduct as a business expense if he or she had paid for it. Examples include a company car for business use and subscriptions to business magazines. Under special rules, all of the use of a demonstrator car by an auto salesperson is excluded if there are substantial restrictions on personal use.

A *frivolous benefit* that is a service for an item of such small value that, after taking into account how frequently similar benefits are provided to employees, makes accounting for the benefit unreasonable or administratively impracticable. Examples include typing of a personal letter by a company secretary, occasional personal use of a company copying machine, occasional parties or picnics for employees, occasional supper money and taxi fare for employees working overtime, holiday gifts with a low fair market value, occasional tickets for entertainment events, and coffee and doughnuts furnished to employees. Also excluded from the employee's income are meals at an eating facility operated by the employer for the employees' benefit on or near the employer's business premises if the income from the facility equals or exceeds the direct operating costs of the facility.

A *qualified transportation benefit*, which includes transit passes, transportation in a commuter highway vehicle to and from work, and qualified parking at or near the place of work. The combined exclusion for the transit passes and transportation cannot exceed $60 per month; the exclusion for parking cannot exceed $160 per month.

A *qualified moving expense reimbursement* which includes any amount received, directly or indirectly by an employee from an employer as a payment for, or reimbursement of, expenses that would be deductible as moving expenses, if paid or incurred by the employee.

An *on-premises* gym or other athletic facility provided and operated by the employer if substantially all the use is by employees, their spouses, and their dependent children.

A *qualified tuition reduction* which an educational organization provides to its employees for education, generally below the graduate level.

SICK PAY

Sick pay generally means any amount paid under a plan because of an employee's temporary absence from work due to injury, sickness, or disability. Sick pay can also be called payments on account of sickness or accident disability. It may be paid by either the employer or a third party, such as an insurance company. Sick pay includes both short- and long-term benefits; it is often expressed as a percentage of the employee's regular wages. Sick pay is usually subject to Social Security, Medicare, and FUTA taxes. Sick pay may also be subject to either mandatory or voluntary federal income tax withholding, depending on who pays it.

A *sick pay plan* is a plan or system established by an employer under which sick pay is available to employees generally or to a class or classes of employees. A plan or system does not exist if benefits are provided on a discretionary or occasional basis with merely a good intention to aid particular employees in time of need. The existence of a plan or system is shown if the plan is in writing, or is otherwise made known to employees, such as by a bulletin board notice or the long and established practice of the employer. Other indications of the existence of a plan or system include, but are not limited to, references to the plan or system in the contract of employment, employer contributions to a plan, and segregated accounts for the payments of benefits.

The requirements for income tax withholding on sick pay and the methods for figuring it differ depending on whether the sick pay is paid by:

1) The employer.
2) An agent of the employee.
3) A third party that is not the employer's agent.

Sick pay paid by the employer or the employer's agent is subject to mandatory income tax withholding. An employer or agent paying sick pay determines the income tax to be withheld based on the employee's Form W-4. The employee cannot choose how much will be withheld. Sick pay paid by an agent is treated as supplemental wages. If the agent does not pay regular wages to the employee, the agent can choose to withhold income tax at a flat 28% rate, rather than at the wage withholding rate. Sick pay paid by a third party that is not the employer's agent is not subject to mandatory income tax withholding. However, an employee can elect to have income tax withheld, and the third party should withhold income tax on all payments of sick pay made 8 or more days after the employee's request. The minimum amount of withholding that the employee can specify is $20 a week.

Special Rules for Paying Taxes

If two or more related corporations employ the same individual at the same time and pay this individual through a common paymaster, which is one of the corporations, the corporations are considered a single employer. They have to pay, in total, no more Social Security and Medicare taxes than a single employer would. Each corporation must pay its own part of the employment taxes and can deduct only its part of the wages. The deductions will not be allowed unless the corporation reimburses the common paymaster for the wage and tax payment.

Third Party Liability for Paying Taxes. Any lender, surety, or other third party who pays wages directly to the employee of another employer, or to the employee's agent, is responsible for any required withholding on those wages. This includes the withholding of income, Social Security, and Medicare taxes. The third party is also liable for any interest and penalties accruing on these accounts. If a third party supplies funds to an employer so that the employer can pay the employee's wages, and if the third party knows that the employer will not pay or deposit the taxes that are required to be withheld when due, then the third party must pay the taxes withheld from the employee's wages, but not paid by the employer. The third party supplier must also pay interest on the taxes if they are paid after the due date of the employer's return.

Third parties are liable only for payment of the employee's part of payroll taxes; they are not liable for the employer's part. The employer must file an employment tax return for wages that he or she or a third party pays, and must furnish statements for employees of wages paid and taxes withheld. The employer also remains liable for any withholding taxes not paid by the third party.

Pensions and Annuities

Pension and annuity payments are subject to federal income tax withholding unless the recipient chooses not to have the taxes withheld. The withholding rules apply to the taxable part of payments from an employer pension, annuity, profit-share, stock bonus, or other deferred compensation plans. The rules also apply to payments from an individual retirement arrangement (IRA), an annuity, endowment, or life insurance contract issued by a life insurance company. There is no withholding on any part of a distribution that is not expected to be includable in the recipient's gross income.

Withholding on Periodic Payments. Periodic payments are payments for more than one year that are not eligible rollover distributions. Periodic payments include substantially equal payments made at least once a year over the life of the employee and/or beneficiaries, or for 10 years or more. For withholding purposes, these payments are treated as if they are wages. They can be figured by using the income tax withholding tables; 10% of a *nonperiodic payment* that is not an eligible rollover distribution should be withheld; 20% of an eligible rollover distribution is withheld, unless the recipient wants to have the distribution paid in a direct rollover to an eligible retirement plan, including an IRA. An eligible rollover distribution is the taxable part of any distribution from a qualified plan or tax-sheltered annuity but *not an IRA* except:

1) One of a series of substantially equal periodic payments made at least annually for the life or life expectancy of the employee and the employee's beneficiary, or for a specified period of 10 years or more.

2) Any part of a distribution that is a minimum distribution required by the tax Code.

Continuous Employment. A term of continuous employment means a single term or two or more following terms of employment with the same employer. A continuous term includes holidays, regular days off, and days off for illness or vacation. A continuous term begins on the first day an employee works for an employer and earns pay. It ends on the earlier of the employee's last workday before the 30-day period. If an employment relationship is ended, the term of continuous employment is ended, even if a new employment relationship is established with the same employer within 30 days.

Chapter 9

Travel, Entertainment, and Gift Expenses

Travel away from home, entertainment, gifts, and local transportation may be tax deductible business related expenses. This discussion explains what expenses are deductible, how to report them on a return, what records must be kept to prove the expenses, and how to treat any expense reimbursements the taxpayer receives.

TRAVEL EXPENSES DEFINED

For tax purposes, travel expenses are ordinary and necessary expenses that are paid while traveling away from home for business, profession, or job responsibilities. An *ordinary* expense is one that is common and accepted in the taxpayer's field of business, trade, or profession. A *necessary* expense is one that is helpful and appropriate to the business. An expense does not have to be indispensable to be considered necessary; however, expenses that are lavish cannot be deducted.

An employee is traveling away from home if:

1) Business related duties require him or her to be away from the general area of the employee's tax home substantially longer than an ordinary day's work.

2) Sleep or rest is needed to meet the demands of the work while away from home.

The rest requirement is not satisfied by merely napping in a car. An employee is not considered to have to be away from the tax home for a whole day or from dusk to dawn as long as relief from duty is long enough to get necessary sleep or rest.

What Is a Tax Home?

To deduct travel expenses, the location of the *tax home* must be determined. A tax home is a regular place of business or post of duty, regardless of where a family home is maintained.

1) A tax home includes an entire city or general area in which the business or work is located.

2) If the individual has more than one regular place of business, the tax home is the main place of business.

3) If the person does not have a regular or a main place of business because of the nature of the work, then the tax home can be placed where the person regularly lives. If the taxpayer does not fit any of these categories, he or she is considered a transient and the tax home is where the person works. As a transient, travel expense deductions cannot be claimed because a transient is never considered to be away from home. A main place of business or work can be determined with the help of the following three factors:

   1) The total time ordinarily spent working in each area.

   2) The degree of business activity in each area.

   3) The amount of income earned in each area.

If a transient worker moves from job to job, maintains no fixed home, and is not associated with any particular business locality, each place becomes a main place of business and the worker's tax home. Expenses for meals and lodging cannot be deducted.

Temporary Assignment or Job

If work or business activity is conducted at a location within the general area of the tax home, and it is not the practice to return home from this location at the end of each day's work, and the assignment or job away from the main place of work is temporary, the tax home does not change. If the person is considered to be away from home for the whole period, travel expenses are deductible. A temporary assignment in a single location is one that is expected to last, and does in fact last, for one year or less. If the assignment or job is indefinite, that location becomes a new tax home and travel expenses cannot be deducted while there. The assignment or job in a single location is considered indefinite if it is expected to last for more than one year, regardless of whether it actually exceeds one year.

A worker must determine when starting work if the assignment is temporary or indefinite. If employment is to last for one year or less, it is temporary in the absence of facts and circumstances that indicate otherwise. Employment that is initially temporary can become indefinite due to changed circumstances. A series of assignments to the same location, all for short periods, but that is together over a long period, can be considered an indefinite assignment.

SOME DEDUCTIBLE TRAVEL EXPENSES

Deductible travel expenses include those ordinary and necessary expenses incurred while traveling away from home on business. The type of expenses that are deductible depends on the facts and circumstances.

Travel by airplane, train, or bus between the home and business destination can be deducted by the amount paid for tickets. The amount deductible for travel by ship can be limited. Taxi, commuter bus, and limousine fares can be deducted when used between the airport or station and the taxpayer's hotel. These fares can also be deducted when going between the home and work location of customers or clients, the business meeting place, or temporary work location. The cost of sightseeing, shopping, or similar nonbusiness activities cannot be deducted. The costs of sending baggage and samples or display materials between the regular workplace location and temporary work location can be deducted. Car expense when traveling away from home on business is deductible in 1996 at the rate of 31 cents per mile, 12 cents per mile for charitable activities, and 10 cents per mile for medical and moving expenses. The cost of leasing a car for business purposes while traveling away from home is deductible, but if the lease is for 30 days or more, the amount may have to be included in the person's income. While the standard mileage rate of 31 cents for 1996 cannot be deducted for leased car usage, actual operation expenses for a leased car are deductible. For a car that the employee owns, a choice can be made between deducting actual business related expenses or claiming the standard mileage rate.

The cost of lodging for overnight business trips and expenses associated with stopping for sleep or rest necessary to properly perform required duties can be deducted. The cost of meals cannot be deducted if it is not necessary to stop for rest. Meal expense includes amounts spent for food, beverages, sales taxes, and tips relating to the meal. Either the actual cost or a standard amount can be deducted. Only 50% of the cost of unreimbursed business-related meals can be deducted. This limit applies whether the unreimbursed meal expense is for business or business entertainment. Expenses for meals cannot be deducted to the extent they are lavish or extravagant. An expense is not considered lavish or extravagant if it is reasonable based on the facts and circumstances associated with the expenditure. Expenses will not be disallowed merely because they are more than a fixed dollar amount, or take place at deluxe restaurants, hotels, nightclubs, or resorts.

Reasonable laundry expenses can be deducted while away from home on business. Telephone expense for the cost of business calls while traveling away from home can be deducted, including the cost of business communication by fax machine or other devices. Similar ordinary and necessary expenses that are related to business travel can be deducted. Such expenses might include the costs of operating and maintaining a house trailer, public stenographer's fees, and computer rental fees. If a spouse, dependent, or other individual goes with the taxpayer on a business trip or to a business convention, his or her travel expenses usually cannot be deducted. Travel expenses can be deducted only for an accompanying individual if that individual:

1) Is the taxpayer's employee.
2) Has a bona fide business purpose for the travel expense.
3) Would otherwise be allowed to deduct the travel expenses.

For a bona fide business purpose to exist, it must be proved that a real business purpose requires the individual's presence. Incidental services such as typing notes or assisting in entertaining customers are not sufficient to warrant a deduction.

STANDARD MEAL ALLOWANCE

A standard amount for daily meals and incidental expenses while traveling away from home on business can be deducted, and is an alternative to the actual cost method as it allows a deduction for a set amount, depending on where the employee travels, instead of keeping records of actual meal expenses. If the standard meal allowance is used, records must still be kept to prove the time, place, and business purposes during travel, and can be used whether an employee or self-employed.

The standard meal allowance cannot be used if the employee is related to the employer. The standard meal allowance can be used whether or a not the employee is reimbursed for traveling expenses. If not reimbursed, or if reimbursed under a nonaccountable plan for meal expense, 50% of the standard meal allowance can be deducted. If the employee is reimbursed under an accountable plan and is deducting amounts that are more than reimbursements, 50% of the excess amount is deductible.

An employee is related to the employer if:

1) The employer is a half-brother, half-sister, brother, sister, spouse, ancestor, or lineal descendant.
2) The employer is a corporation in which the employee owns, directly or indirectly, more than 10% in value of the outstanding stock.
3) Certain fiduciary relationships exist between the employee and employer involving grantors, trusts, and beneficiaries.

The standard meal allowance is $25 a day for most areas in the United States. Other locations in the United States are designated as high-cost areas, qualifying for higher standard meal allowances. The daily rate for the high cost areas are $30, $34, and $38 for travel on or after January 1, 1995. If travel is to more than one location in one day, the rate in effect for the area where the employee stops to sleep or rest is used.

Standard meal allowance rates do not apply to travel in Alaska, Hawaii, or any other locations outside the continental United States. The federal per diem rates for these locations are published monthly in the *Maximum Travel Per Diem Allowances for Foreign Areas*. (Employers usually have these rates available.) The standard meal allowance cannot be used to prove the amount of meals for traveling for medical or charitable purposes.

BUSINESS, VACATION, OR BOTH?

All travel expenses can be deducted if a trip was entirely business related. While at the business destination, if the employee extended the stay for a vacation, made a nonbusiness side trip, or had other nonbusiness activities, the business related travel expenses include the travel costs of getting to and from the business destination and any business related expenses at the business destination. The cost of meals is subject to the 50% limit on meals. If the trip was solely for personal reasons, such as a vacation, the entire cost of the trip is a nondeductible personal expense; however, any expenses can be deducted while at the destination that are directly related to business. A trip to a resort or on a cruise ship can be a vacation even if the promoter advertises that it is primarily for business. The scheduling of incidental business activities, such as attending lectures, will not change what is, in fact, a vacation into a business trip

TRAVEL OUTSIDE THE UNITED STATES

If any part of business travel is outside the United States, some of the deductions for the cost of getting to and from the employee's destination may be limited. For this purpose, the United States includes the 50 states and the District of Columbia. How much of the travel expenses that can be deducted depends in part upon how much of the trip outside the U.S., was business related. If the entire time of travel outside the U.S. was business related, all travel expenses of getting to and from the business destination are deductible. Even if the entire time was not spent on business activities and the trip was considered entirely for business, all of the business related travel expenses can be deducted if at least one of the following four conditions is met:

1) The employee did not have substantial control over arranging the trip.
    a) The employee is considered not to have substantial control over the trip if the employee was reimbursed or paid a travel expense allowance.
    b) The employee is not related to the employer.
    c) The employee is not a managing executive. *A managing executive* is an employee who has the authority and responsibility, without being subject to the veto of another, to decide on the need for the business travel. A self-employed person is regarded as having substantial control over arranging business trips.
2) The employee was outside the U.S. for a week or less, combining business and nonbusiness activities. One week means seven consecutive days. In counting days, the day the employee left the U.S. is not counted, but the day of return to the U.S. is counted.
3) The employee was outside the U.S. for more than a week, but less than 25% of the total time was spent on nonbusiness activities. For this purpose, both the day the trip began and the day it ended are counted.
4) If it can be established that a personal vacation was not a major consideration, even though the employee has substantial control over arranging the trip, all of the business related expenses are deductible.

COUNTING BUSINESS DAYS

Any day spent traveling to or from a business destination is counted as a business day. If, because of a nonbusiness activity, the employee does not travel by a direct route, the business days are the days it would take to travel a reasonably direct route to the business destination. Extra days for side trips or nonbusiness activities cannot be counted as business days. A business day can be counted for any day that presence is required at a particular place for a specific business purpose, even if most of the day is spent on nonbusiness activities. If the principal activity during working hours is for the trade or business, the day is counted as a business day. Any day that the employee is prevented from working because of circumstances beyond the employee's control is counted as a business day. Weekends, holidays, and other necessary standby days are counted as business days if they fall between business days. If they follow a business meeting or activity and the employee remains at the business destination for nonbusiness or personal reasons, they are not business days. If he or she had a vacation or other nonbusiness activity between the U.S. and the business destination, or between the business destination and the U.S., expenses must be allocated between business and nonbusiness days.

LUXURY WATER TRAVEL

Deduction is limited to twice the federal per diem rate allowable at the time of the travel. For purposes of this limit, the federal per diem is the highest amount allowed as a daily allowance for living expenses to employees of the executive branch of the federal government while they are away from home but in the United States. If the expenses for luxury water travel include separately stated amounts for meals or entertainment, those amounts are subject to the 50% limit on meals and entertainment before the daily limit is applied.

CONVENTIONS

Travel expenses for attending a convention can be deducted if it can be shown that attendance benefits the person's trade or business. The travel expenses cannot be deducted for one's family. If the convention is for investment, political, social, or other purposes unrelated to the person's trade or business, the expenses are not deductible. Nonbusiness expenses, such as social or sightseeing expenses, are personal expenses and are not deductible. The agenda of the convention does not have to deal specifically with the official duties or the responsibilities of the attendee's position or business. It is enough if the agenda is related to an active trade or business and its responsibilities so that attendance for a business purpose is justified.

Expenses cannot be deducted for attending a convention, or similar meetings held outside the North American area, unless the meeting is directly related to a trade or business. It must be as reasonable to hold the meeting outside North America as in it. If the meeting meets these requirements, the rules for deducting expenses must be satisfied for business in general for travel outside the United States. The following factors must be taken into account to determine if it is reasonable to hold a meeting outside North America:

1) The purpose of the meeting and the activities taking place at the meeting.
2) The purposes and activities of the sponsoring organizations or groups.

3) The residences of the active members of the sponsoring organization and the places at which other meetings of the sponsoring organizations or groups have been or will be held.

4) Other relevant factors: Up to $2,000 per year of the expenses of attending conventions, seminars, or similar meetings held on cruise ships can be deducted. It must be established that meetings are directly related to a trade or business.

All ships that sail are considered cruise ships. Cruise ship expenses can be deducted if all of the following are true:

1) The cruise ship is a vessel registered in the United States.

2) All of the cruise ship's ports of call are located in the U.S. or in possessions of the U.S.

3) A written statement signed by the attendee is attached to his or her tax return that includes the total days of the trip, the number of hours each day devoted to scheduled business activities, and a program of the scheduled business activities of the meeting.

4) A written statement signed by an officer of the organization or group sponsoring the meeting that includes:

   a) A schedule of the business activities of each day of the meeting.

   b) The number of hours the participant attended the scheduled business activities.

ENTERTAINMENT EXPENSES

Business related expenses can be deducted for entertaining a client, customer, or employee. To be deductible, the expenses must be both ordinary and necessary. An ordinary expense is one that is common and accepted in the particular field of business, trade, or profession. A necessary expense is one that is helpful and appropriate for the business. An expense does not have to be indispensable to be considered necessary. In addition, the entertainment expense must meet one of two tests:

1) Directly related test.

2) Associated test.

Even if all requirements for claiming a deduction for entertainment expenses are met, the amount that can be deducted can be limited. Usually, 50% of unreimbursed entertainment expenses can be deducted.

The entertainment can be proved as directly related by showing that a substantial business discussion was engaged in during the entertainment. If the expenses do not meet the directly related test, they may meet the associated test. To meet the associated test for entertainment expenses, including entertainment related meals, it must be shown that the entertainment is associated with a trade or business and that it directly precedes or follows a substantial business discussion. Any ordinary and necessary expense is associated with the active conduct of a trade or business if it can be shown that the entertainer had a clear business purpose for having the expense. The purpose may be to get new business or to encourage the continuation of an existing business relationship. If part of the entertainment expense is for persons not closely connected with the guests who attended the substantial business discussion, that part of the expense would not qualify for the association test.

Whether a business discussion is substantial depends on all the facts of each case. It must be shown that the participants in the discussion were actively engaged in the meeting, negotiation, or other business transactions to get income or some other specific business benefit. The meeting does not have to be for any specified length of time, but it must be shown that the business discussion was substantial in relation to the meal or entertainment. It is not necessary that more time be devoted to business than to entertainment. Business need not be discussed during the meal or entertainment.

A substantial business discussion is considered to have taken place at a convention if the meetings are attended, or a trade or business meeting is sponsored and conducted by a business or professional organization. However, the convention or meeting must be attended to further a trade or business, and the organization that sponsors the convention or meeting must schedule a program of business activities that is the main activity of the convention or meeting. The cost of entertainment for spouses or for spouses of business customers—unless it can be shown that there was a clear business purpose, rather than a personal or social purpose for providing the entertainment—is not a business expense.

CLUB DUES AND MEMBERSHIP FEES

An employee is not allowed a deduction for dues, including initiation fees, for membership in any club, organization for business, pleasure, recreation, or other social purpose. This applies to any membership organization, if one of the principal purposes is to conduct entertainment activities for members or their guests, or to provide members or their guests with access to entertainment facilities. The purposes and activities of a club, not its name, will determine whether or not the dues are deductible. Not deductible are dues paid to country clubs, golf and athletic clubs, airline clubs, hotel clubs, and clubs operated to provide meals that are considered to be conducive to business discussions.

WHAT ENTERTAINMENT EXPENSES ARE DEDUCTIBLE?

Entertainment includes any activity considered to provide entertainment, amusement, or recreation. Examples include entertaining guests at nightclubs, at social, athletic, and sporting clubs, at theaters, sporting events, on yachts, or on business, fishing, vacation, and similar trips. Entertainment also can include meeting personal, living, or family needs of individuals such as providing meals, a hotel suite, or a car for business customers or their families. Entertainment includes the cost of a meal provided to a customer or client, whether the meal is a part of other entertainment or by itself. To deduct an entertainment related meal, the employer or employee must be present when the food or beverages are provided.

The kind of business will determine if a particular activity constitutes entertainment. Expenses are not deductible when a group of business acquaintances take turns picking up each other's meal or entertainment checks without regard to whether any business purposes are served.

Entertainment expenses that are directly related to and necessary for attending business meetings or conventions of certain exempt organizations can be deducted. These organizations include business leagues, chambers of commerce, real estate boards, trade associations, and professional associations. The expenses for attendance must be related to a trade or business and are subject to the 50% limit on entertainment expenses.

SKYBOXES AND OTHER PRIVATE LUXURY BOXES

Restrictions apply to the amount of entertainment expense that can be deducted for the rental of skyboxes and other private luxury boxes for more than one event at the same sports arena. Even if the restrictions do not apply, the deduction is generally subject to the 50% limit on entertainment expenses.

In determining whether a skybox has been rented for more than one event, each game or other performance counts as one event. Renting a skybox for series games, such as the World Series, counts as renting it for more than one event. In addition, all skyboxes that are rented in the same arena, along with any rentals by related parties, are considered in making this determination. Related parties include:

1) Family member; i.e, spouses, ancestors, and lineal descendants.
2) Parties who have made a reciprocal arrangement involving the sharing of skyboxes.
3) Related corporations.
4) A partnership and its principal partners.

5) A corporation and a partnership with common ownership.

If a skybox is rented for more than one event, the deduction is limited to the price of a regular nonluxury box seat ticket. If expenses for food and beverages are separately stated, these expenses can be deducted in addition to the amounts allowable for the skybox, subject to the requirements and limits that apply. The amounts separately stated for food and beverages must be reasonable. The charges cannot be inflated for food and beverages to circumvent the limited deduction for skybox rentals.

To meet the directly related test for entertainment expenses, including entertainment related meals:

1) The main purpose of the combined business and entertainment was the active conduct of business.
2) The employer or employee did engage in business with the person during the entertainment period.
3) The entertainer had more than a general expectation of getting income or some other specific business benefit at some future time.

Business is not considered to be the main purpose when business and entertainment are combined on hunting or fishing trips, or on yachts or other pleasure boats, unless the purpose can be shown to be otherwise. Even if business was the main purpose, expenses cannot be deducted for the use of an entertainment facility.

All the facts must be considered including the nature of the business transacted and the reasons for conducting business during the entertainment. It is not necessary to devote more time to business than to entertainment. However, if the business discussion is only incidental to the entertainment, it is not directly related. If the entertainment takes place in a business setting and is for business or work, the expenses are considered directly related to the business or work. The following situations are examples of entertainment in a business setting:

1) Entertainment in a hospitality room at a convention where business goodwill is created through the display or discussion of business products.
2) Entertainment that is mainly a price rebate on the sale of products.
3) Entertainment of a business nature occurring under circumstances where there is no meaningful personal or social relationship between the entertainer and the persons entertained.

Expenses are not considered directly related when entertainment occurs where, because of substantial distractions, there is little or no possibility of engaging in the active conduct of a business. Examples are:

1) A meeting or discussion at a nightclub, theater, or sporting event.
2) A meeting or discussion during a social gathering.
3) A meeting with a group that includes persons who are not business associates at places such as cocktail lounges, country clubs, golf clubs, athletic clubs, or vacation resorts.

THE 50% LIMIT

Only 50% of business related meal and entertainment expenses can be deducted. This limit applies to employees and employers and to self-employed persons, including independent contractors, or their clients, depending on whether the expenses are reimbursed. The 50% limit applies to business meals and entertainment expenses incurred while:

1) Traveling away from home on business.
2) Entertaining business customers at the entertainer's place of business, a restaurant, or other location.
3) Attending a business convention or reception, business meeting, or business luncheon at a club.

Taxes and tips relating to a business meal or entertainment activity are included in the amount that is subject to the 50% limit. Expenses such as cover charges for admission to a nightclub, rent paid for a room in which a dinner or cocktail party is held, or the amount paid for parking at a sports arena are subject to the 50% limit. However, the cost of transportation to and from a business meal or a business related entertainment activity is not subject to the 50% limit.

If an expense is incurred for goods and services consisting of meals, entertainment, and other services such as lodging or transportation, the expenses must be allocated between the cost of meals and entertainment and the cost of other services. There must be a reasonable basis for making the allocation.

APPLICATION OF THE 50% LIMIT

The 50% limit on meal and entertainment expenses applies if the expense is otherwise deductible, and also applies to activities that are not trade or business related. The limit applies to meal and entertainment expenses incurred for the production of income, including rental or royalty income. It also applies to the cost of meals included in deductible educational expenses. The 50% limit is applied after determining the amount that would otherwise qualify for a deduction. After the amount of meal and entertainment expenses has been determined the limit is then applied. The 2% of adjusted gross income limit must then be applied.

The 50% limit on meal and entertainment expense does not apply if the expense meets one of the following exceptions:

1) If the employee is reimbursed by his or her employer under an accountable plan and does not treat the reimbursement as wages. To be an accountable plan, an employer's reimbursement or allowance arrangement must include all three of the following rules:

   a) The expenses must have a business connection. Deductible expenses must have been paid or incurred while performing services as an employee of the employer.

   b) The expenses must have been adequately accounted for to an employer within a reasonable period of time.

   c) Any excess reimbursement or allowance must be returned to an employer within a reasonable period of time.

2) For self-employed persons, deductible meal and entertainment expenses are subject to the 50% limit. However, the expenses are not subject to the 50% limit if they are incurred as an independent contractor.

   a) The customer or client reimburses an independent contractor, allowing him or her an allowance for expenses in connection with services performed.

   b) Adequate records of expenses are furnished to the customer or client, who are, however, subject to the 50% limit if the independent contractor's expenses are otherwise deductible.

3) The cost of meals, entertainment, or recreational facilities to the general public can be deducted as a means of advertising or promoting goodwill in the community.

4) The costs can be deducted for providing meals, entertainment, goods and services, or use of facilities that are actually sold to the public.

BUSINESS GIFT EXPENSES

No more than $25 can be deducted for business gifts given directly or indirectly to any one person during his or her tax year. A gift to a company that is intended for the eventual personal use or benefit of a particular person or a limited class of people is considered an indirect gift to that particular person, or to the individuals within that class of people who receive the gift. A gift to the spouse of a business customer or client is an indirect gift to the customer or client. Incidental costs, such as engraving on jewelry, packaging, insuring, and mailing, are not included in determining the cost of a gift for purposes of the $25 limit. A related cost is considered incidental only if it does not add substantial value to the gift.

The following items are not included in the $25 limit for business gifts:

1) An item that costs four dollars or less and has the giver's name clearly and permanently imprinted on the gift, and is one of a number of identical items the giver widely distributes—pens, desk sets, plastic bags, and cases.

2) Signs, display racks, or other promotional material to be used on the business premises of the recipient.

Any item that might be considered either a gift or an entertainment expense generally will be considered an entertainment expense; customer-packaged food or beverages that are intended for a customer or client to use at a later date are treated as a gift expense.

COMMUTING AND LOCAL TRANSPORTATION EXPENSES

Commuting expenses cannot be deducted no matter how far away from home the regular place of work is. Parking fees at the workplace are nondeductible commuting expenses, but are deductible when visiting a customer or client. Transportation expenses necessary to go between home and a part time job on a day off from the main job are commuting expenses and cannot be deducted. If an employee has one or more regular places of business and commutes to a temporary work location, expenses are deductible for the daily round-trip transportation between a residence and the temporary location. The temporary work must be irregular or short-term, which is considered a matter of days or weeks. If the temporary work location is beyond the general area of the regular place of work and requires overnight stays, the travel is a deductible travel away-from-home expense.

If a person does not have a regular place of work, but ordinarily works at different locations in a metropolitan area where the worker lives, daily transportation costs between home and a temporary work site outside the metropolitan area can be deducted. A metropolitan area includes the area in the city limits and the suburbs that are considered part of that metropolitan area. Nondeductible daily transportation costs are those between the home and temporary work sites within the worker's metropolitan area.

Local transportation expenses include the ordinary and necessary expenses of getting from one workplace to another in the course of a business day when the taxpayer is traveling within his or her home area. Local transportation rules apply when a regular or main job requires being away from home and includes the cost of getting from home to a temporary workplace(s). The temporary workplace can be either within the area of the home or outside that area. Local business transportation does not include expenses while traveling away from home overnight, which are deductible as travel expenses.

Local business transportation expenses include the cost of transportation by air, rail, bus, taxi, and the cost of driving and maintaining the employee's car. The expenses for local transportation can be deducted if they are ordinary and necessary.

If the employee works at two places in a day, and for the same employer, expenses can be deducted for getting from one workplace to the other. If for some reason the worker does not go directly from one location to the other, only the amount it costs to go directly from the first location to the second can be deducted.

RECORD KEEPING

Records must be kept when planning to deduct expenses in order to have accurate information to show the IRS if a tax return is ever examined. An employer, as well, may require proof of expenses for reimbursed expenses under an accountable plan. The taxpayer must be able to prove deductions for travel, entertainment, business gift, and local transportation expenses. The records must be precisely accurate; estimates or approximations do not qualify as proof of an expense. The elements of every expense need not be shown, but a record of the elements of an expense of a business transaction made at or near the time of the expense, and supported by sufficient documentary evidence, has more value than a statement prepared later when there can be a lack of accurate recall. A log maintained on a weekly basis which accounts for the expense or use during the week is considered a record made at or near the time of the expense or use. An expense account statement given to the employer, client, or customer is considered to have been made at or near the time of the expense or use. The statement must be copied from the taxpayer's account book, diary, statement of expenses, or similar record.

HOW TO PROVE EXPENSES

Expenses can be deducted only if they can be proved. Amounts of expenses cannot be deducted if they are approximated or estimated or amounts that are considered lavish or extravagant. A receipt is ordinarily the best evidence to prove the amount of an expense. To deduct travel expenses, the following four elements must be verified:

1) Each separate amount spent for travel away from home must be listed and proved. If reimbursement is on per diem allowance payments, proof may not be needed of separate amounts spent for meals, lodging, or incidental expenses.

2) The dates when an employee left and returned home for each trip, as well as the number of days spent on business while traveling away from home must be shown.

3) The area of travel's destination must be shown and described by the name of the city, town, or similar designation.

4) The business reason for travel or the business benefit gained must be shown.

PROOF OF ENTERTAINMENT EXPENSES

To deduct entertainment expenses, including entertainment-related meals, the following six elements must be proved:

1) The amount of each separate entertainment expense. Incidental items, such as taxi fares and telephone calls can be totaled on a daily basis.

2) The date that entertainment took place.

3) The name, address or location, and the type of entertainment, such as dinner or theater, if the information is not apparent from the name of the place.

4) The business reason for the entertainment, or the business benefit gained or expected to be gained, and the nature of any business discussion or activity that took place.

5) The occupation or other information about the person or persons for whom the entertainment expense is being claimed. Name, title, or other designation sufficient to establish the business relationship to the taxpayer should be included.

6) The presence of the employer or employee at a business meal given for a client.

If a large number of people are entertained, each person's name in a readily identifiable group of people does not have to be recorded; it is enough to designate the class. To deduct the cost of meals or entertainment directly before or after a business discussion, the taxpayer must be able to prove the date, place, and duration of the business discussion, as well as the nature of the business discussion and the business reason for the entertainment or the business benefit gained, and to identify the people who participated in both the business discussion and in the entertainment activity.

Proof of Gift Expenses

To deduct gift expenses, the following five elements must be proved:

1) The cost of the gift.

2) The date the gift was given.

3) A description of the gift.

4) The reason for giving the gift or the business benefit gained from giving it.

5) The occupation or other information about the person receiving the gift, including name, title, or other designation to establish his or her business relationship to the giver.

Proof of Local Business Transportation Expenses

To deduct local business transportation expenses, the following four elements must be proved.

1) The cost of the transportation.

2) The date of the transportation.

3) The business destination.

4) The reason for the expense, unless the business purpose, such as the sales route, is clear from the surrounding circumstances.

Additional Record Keeping Rule

Each separate payment for an expense is considered a separate expense. If a customer or client is entertained at dinner and then goes to the theater, the dinner expense and the cost of the theater tickets are two separate expenses and must be recorded separately in the taxpayer's records. There can be one daily entry for reasonable categories of expenses, such as taxi fares, telephone calls, or other incidental travel costs. Meals should be in a separate category, including tips with the costs of services received. Expenses of a similar nature, occurring during the course of a single event, are considered a single expense.

Documentary evidence, such as receipts, canceled checks, or bills, are required as evidence of support for claimed expenses. This evidence is not needed, however, if:

1) Expenses for meals and lodging expenses while traveling away from home are accounted for to the employer under an unaccountable plan, and a per diem allowance method is used that includes meals and lodging.

2) For expenses, other than lodging, that are less than $75.

3) For a transportation expense for which a receipt is not readily available.

Documentary evidence ordinarily will be considered adequate if it shows the amount, date, place, and essential character of the expense.

A hotel receipt is enough to support expenses for business travel if it has:

1) The name and location of the hotel.

2) The dates of the stay.

3) Separate amounts for charges such as lodging, meals, and incidentals.

A restaurant receipt is sufficient evidence for business meals if it has the name and location of the restaurant, the number of people served, and the date and amount of the expense. The receipt must show any items other than for food and beverages.

Canceled checks, together with bills from the payees, ordinarily establish the cost of business expense items. However, a canceled check by itself does not prove a business expense without other evidence to show that it was in fact for a business purpose. A written statement of the business purpose of an expense item is needed, however, and the degree of proof varies according to the circumstances in each case. If the business purpose of an expense is clear from the surrounding circumstances, a written explanation is not needed.

CONFIDENTIAL INFORMATION

Confidential information relating to an element of a deduction expense need not be put in an account book, diary, or other record, but the information has to be recorded elsewhere at or near the time of the expense and be available to fully prove that element of the expense. If the total cost of travel or entertainment is claimed but it cannot be proved how much it cost for each person, the cost must be divided among the taxpayer and his or her guests if such a determination is necessary. To do so, the total cost is divided by the total number of persons; the result is the amount used to figure the deductible expenses for each qualifying person. If a taxpayer's records are inadequate to prove an element of expense, then the element must be proved by:

1) The taxpayer's own statement, whether written or oral, that contains specific information about the element.

2) Other supporting evidence that is sufficient to establish the element.

If the element is the description of a gift, or the cost, time, place, or date of an expense, there must be direct evidence. The evidence can be a written statement, or the oral testimony of the taxpayer's guests or a witness, which gives detailed information about the element or documentary evidence. If the element is either the business relationship of the guests or the business purpose of the amount spent, the evidence can be circumstantial. Other evidence can be allowed if, because of the nature of the situation in which an expense is made, the taxpayer cannot get a receipt.

This approach applies if all of the following are true:

1) It was not possible to obtain evidence for an element of the expense or use that conforms fully to the adequate records requirements.

2) It was not possible to obtain evidence for an element that conforms fully to the rules under inadequate records.

3) Other evidence is presented for the element that is the best proof possible under the circumstances.

In this case, such other evidence is considered to satisfy the substantiation requirements. If a deduction can be proved by reconstructing claimed expenses, or if receipts and other documentation cannot be produced for reasons beyond the taxpayer's control, additional information might have to be provided to the IRS to clarify or to establish the accuracy or reliability of information contained in records, statements, testimony, or documentary evidence before a deduction is allowed.

Proof to support a claim to a deduction must be kept as long as an income tax return can be examined. It will usually be necessary to keep records for three years from the date the income tax return on which the deduction is claimed is filed. A return filed early is considered as filed on the due date. Employees who give their records and documentation to their employers and are reimbursed for their expenses do not have to keep duplicate copies of this information. However, proof of expenses will have to be provided if:

1) Deductions are claimed for expenses that are more than reimbursements.

2) When expenses are reimbursed under a nonaccountable plan.

3) The expense payer does not use adequate accounting procedures to verify expense accounts.

4) The taxpayer is related to his or her employer.

REIMBURSEMENTS

A reimbursement or other expense allowance arrangement is a system or plan that an employer can use to pay, substantiate, and recover the expenses, advances, or reimbursements and amounts charged to the employer for employee business expenses. It can also be a system used to keep track of amounts an employee receives from the employer's agent or a third party. Arrangements include per diem and mileage allowances. If a single payment includes both wages and an expense reimbursement, the amount of the reimbursement must be specifically identified. An employer has the following different options for reimbursing employees for business related travel expenses:

1) Reimbursements for the actual expenses.

2) Using the meals only allowance to reimburse meal expenses and incidental expenses and reimbursing the employee for actual lodging expenses.

3) Using the high-low method. This is a simplified method of computing the federal per diem rate for travel within the continental United States. It eliminates the need to keep a current list of the per diem rate in effect for each city in the U.S. The per diem amount for travel differs in different areas of the country and is available from the IRS. The federal per diem rate allowed and the incidental expense rate is for a full 24-hour day of travel.

4) Reimbursing the employee under any other method that is acceptable to the IRS.

5) Using the regular federal per diem rate.

The employer should tell an employee what method of reimbursement is used and what records the employee must submit. If an employee is not reimbursed or given an allowance for expenses and is paid a salary or commission with the understanding that the employee will pay the expenses, the employee has no reimbursement or allowance arrangement and must deduct his or her own expenses on the tax return. If an employer reimburses employees' business expenses, how the employer treats expense reimbursement depends in part on whether the system is an accountable plan. Reimbursements treated as paid under an accountable plan are not reported as compensation. Reimbursements treated as paid under nonaccountable plans are reported as compensation.

REASONABLE PERIOD OF TIME—A DEFINITION

The definition of a reasonable period of time depends on the facts of the taxpayer's particular situation. The IRS will consider the time to be reasonable if the taxpayer:

1) Receives an advance within 30 days of the time the expense has been incurred.

2) Adequately accounts for the employees expenses within 60 days after they were paid or incurred.

3) Returns any excess reimbursement within 120 days after the expense was paid or incurred.

If an employee is given a periodic statement, at least quarterly, that asked him or her to either return or adequately account for outstanding advances and the employee complies within 120 days of the statement, the IRS will consider the amount adequately accounted for or returned within a reasonable period of time.

PROVING EXPENSES WITH A PER DIEM ALLOWANCE

If an employer pays for expenses using a per diem allowance, including a meals-only allowance, the allowance can be used as proof for the amount of expenses claimed. However, the amount of expense that can be proven this way cannot be more than the regular federal per diem rate or the high-low method. The per diem allowance can only be used as proof of the cost of meals and/or lodging under the adequate accounting requirements. Other proof must be provided of the time, place, and business purpose for each expense. The regular federal per diem rate is the highest amount that the federal government will pay to its employees for lodging, meal, and incidental expenses while they are traveling away from home in a particular area. The rates are different for different locations, and the rate in effect for the area where the employee stops for sleep or rest must be used.

RETURNING EXCESS REIMBURSEMENTS

Under an accountable plan, any excess reimbursement or other expense allowance for business expenses must be returned to the person paying the reimbursement or allowance. Excess reimbursement means any amount for which the employee did not adequately account within a reasonable period of time. For example, if an employee receives a travel advance and did not spend all the money on business related expenses, or the employee does not have proof of all his or her expenses, then there is an excess reimbursement.

If an employer provides an expense allowance before the employee actually has the expense, and the allowance is reasonably calculated not to exceed expected expenses, the employee has received a *travel advance*. Under an accountable plan, the employee must be required to adequately account to the employer for the advance and be required to return any excess within a reasonable period of time. If the employee does not adequately account for or does not return any excess advance within a reasonable period of time, the amount is not accounted for or has not been returned within a reasonable period of time will be treated as having been paid under a nonaccountable plan.

UNPROVEN AMOUNTS

If the employee cannot prove actual travel on each day for which a per diem allowance was paid, the unproven amount of the travel advance must be returned within a reasonable period of time. If the excess reimbursement is not returned, the employee must report the unproven amount of per diem as income, and the employer reports the amount on the employee's Form W-2. If an employer's per diem plan or similar allowance is higher than the federal rate, the employee does not have to return the difference between the two rates for the period of proven business related travel expenses, and the difference is reported on the Form W-2.

NONACCOUNTABLE PLANS

A nonaccountable plan is a reimbursement or expense allowance arrangement that does not meet the rules for Accountable Plans. In addition, the following payments made under an accountable plan will be treated as paid under a nonaccountable plan:

1) Excess reimbursements that were not returned to the employer.
2) Reimbursements of nondeductible expenses related to the employer's business.

An arrangement that repays an employee for business expenses by reducing the amount reported as wages, salary, or other compensation will be treated as a nonaccountable plan. This is because the employee is entitled to receive the full amount of compensation regardless of whether the employee incurred any business expenses. The employer will combine the amount of any reimbursement or other expense allowance paid to an employee under a nonaccountable plan with wages, salary, or other compensation, and the employer will report the total on the employee's Form W-2. The employee must report expenses on Form 1040 with meal and entertainment expenses subject to the 50% limit, and total expenses subject to the 2% of adjusted gross income limit that applies to most miscellaneous itemized deductions.

RULES FOR INDEPENDENT CONTRACTORS

Reimbursement or an allowance for meals, travel, entertainment, or gift expenses incurred by an independent contractor on behalf of a client, requires that adequate accounting of the expenses should be provided to the client. Adequate records of these expenses must be kept regardless of whether they are accounted for to the client. The independent contractor is subject to the 50% limit on the expenses.

If the contractor does adequately account to the client for entertainment expenses, the client or customer must keep records documenting each element of the expenses. If entertainment expenses are accounted for separately, they are subject to the 50% limit on entertainment. The client does not have to file an information return to report the amount for which the contractor was reimbursed, as long as the contractor adequately accounted to the client for these expenses.

If the contractor does not adequately account to the client for allowances or reimbursement of entertainment expenses, then the client or customer need not keep separate records of these items. The client can deduct the reimbursements or allowances as compensation if they are ordinary and necessary business expenses. The client must report amounts paid to a contractor if the total of the reimbursements and any other fees is $600 or more during the calendar year.

Chapter 10

Household Employer Taxes (Nanny Tax)

If a taxpayer has a household employee in 1996, he or she may need to pay federal as well as state employment taxes. There have been problems and misunderstandings for many taxpayers regarding the tax treatment of domestic workers; e.g., a maid, private nurse, health aide, nanny, housekeeper, baby sitter, cook, yard care worker, chauffeur, companion, and the like. In November, 1995, the IRS, issued clear reporting rulings and instructions to help taxpayers decide whether or not a household worker is a household employee, and whether or not the taxpayer needs to pay federal employment taxes. Household employers must report wages of $1,000, or more, paid after 1994.

The following discussion will help taxpayers understand how to decide if a worker is a household employee, how to report federal unemployment tax, Social Security tax, Medicare tax, federal income tax withholding, and what records should be retained by the taxpayer.

WHO IS A HOUSEHOLD EMPLOYEE?

The first consideration is whether or not the worker is an employee of the householder. Essentially, if the taxpayer controls what work is done and how it is done, such a worker is an employee of the taxpayer. It does not matter whether the work is full-time or part-time, or that the worker was hired through an agency or from a list provided by an agency or association, nor does it matter whether the worker is paid on an hourly, daily, or weekly basis, or by the job. If an agency provides the worker and controls what work is done, and how it is done, the worker is not an employee of the taxpayer. However, if the worker can only control *how* the work is done, the worker is not an employee, but rather is self-employed; i.e., an independent contractor; so the filing requirements may not apply. A self-employed worker usually provides his own tools and offers services to the general public in an independent business.

It is unlawful to knowingly hire or continue to employ an alien who cannot legally work in the United States. When a household employee is hired to work on a regular basis, he or she must complete the employee part of the Immigration and Naturalization Service (INS) form, *Employment Eligibility Verification*. The taxpayer must verify that the employee is either a U.S. citizen or an alien who can legally work. The employer completes his or her part of the form and keeps the completed form.

CASH WAGES

Cash wages include wages paid with checks, money orders, etc. Cash wages do not include the value of food, lodging, clothing, and other noncash items given to household employees. (Cash to reimburse employees in place of these items is included in cash wages.) If the employee is paid for commuting expenses by public transit, the reimbursement up to $65 per month is not counted as wages. The employee's share of Social Security and Medicare taxes should be withheld. It is permissible for the employer to pay the employee's Social Security and Medicare taxes and not have to withhold them from the employee's wages, but the amount the employer pays must be included in the employee's wages for income tax purposes, but are not counted as Social Security and Medicare wages or as federal unemployment (FUTA) wages.

FUTA

The federal unemployment tax is part of the federal and state program under FUTA. As with most employers, household employers pay both the unemployment tax and a state unemployment tax, but it is possible to owe only the FUTA tax or only the state unemployment tax. To find out whether the state unemployment tax is owed, consult the state's unemployment tax agency. The FUTA tax is (currently) 6.2% of the employee's FUTA wages; it is reduced to 0.8% for 1996 if the FUTA wage paid is not more than the wages that are subject to a state unemployment tax, and all the required contributions for 1996 are paid to the taxpayer's state unemployment fund by April 15, 1997. The FUTA tax cannot be withheld from the employee's wages; it must be paid by the employer.

Earned Income Credit (EIC)

When the employer's tax return is filed, the federal employment taxes on the wages paid to the household employee are added, less any advance earned credit payments made to the employee. Earned income credit (EIC) must be an advance payment if the employee gives the employer a properly completed form for the *Earned Income Credit Advance Payment Certificate.* Any advance EIC payments made to the employee reduce the amount of Social Security and Medicare taxes and withheld federal income tax needed to be paid to the IRS. Household employee wages are not required to be withheld by the employer. The tax on a household employee's wages are withheld only if the employee asks the employer to withhold and the employer agrees—a mutual understanding. The federal income tax withholding is calculated on both cash and noncash wages that are paid. Wages paid in any form other than cash are measured by the values of the noncash items. Meals and lodging provided in the home for the taxpayer's convenience are *not* required to be counted as wages. CPAs must sign form 1040 tax returns with domestic employee information. This includes Schedule H, which places much of the compliance burden on the CPA preparer. A CPA who already knows that his or her client has not complied with the revenue laws must promptly advise the client of this fact. The CPA should advise the client of the non-compliance to prevent the client from later pleading ignorance of the requirement.

Employment tax records must be kept for at least four years after the due date of the return when the taxes are reported, or the date the taxes were paid, whichever is later.

Chapter 11

The Securities and Exchange Commission: Private Securities Litigation Reform Act of 1995

To reduce the number of frivolous class action lawsuits, Congress passed the Private Securities Litigation Reform Act of 1995 (the Act). The Act revises the securities laws that professional investors and class action lawyers have used against corporations, accountants, and securities underwriters to win billions of dollars in damages. A safe harbor provision now protects companies from the legal liability for forecasts that subsequently proved to be incorrect, as well as for statements that were inaccurate when they were made. Key personnel of a large number of national CPA firms and various state CPA associations urged members of Congress to support reforms in the bill; the passage of the bill is considered to be significantly helpful to business corporations and the accounting and investment banking professions. The new law encourages the dissemination of forward-looking information and forecasts, using easily understood language that lessens the possibility of frivolous lawsuits by the users of financial statements. The Act's fundamental purpose is to address concerns, raised in a number of Congressional hearings over a four-year period, that the securities litigation system was misaligned in a way that overcompensated weak cases to the detriment of strong cases, and that served investor interests poorly. As the Statement of Managers accompanying the Conference Report explained:

The private securities litigation system is too important to the integrity of American capital markets to allow this system to be undermined by those who seek to line their own pockets by bringing abusive lawsuits. Private securities litigation is an indispensable tool with which defrauded investors can recover their losses without having to rely upon government action. Such private lawsuits promote public and global confidence in our capital markets, help to deter wrongdoing, and guarantee that corporate officers, auditors, directors, lawyers, and others perform their jobs properly. This legislation seeks to return the securities litigation system to that high standard.

PROVISIONS OF THE ACT

The following are some of the Act's provisions:

1) The Act implements a system of proportionate liability in which peripheral defendants pay only their fair share of a judgment. Less accountable defendants will pay a proportionate share of the damages, but parties that knowingly engage in fraudulent actions are still subject to the fullest extent of joint and several liability. Proponents of the bill argued that joint and several liability in the previous law caused plaintiffs' lawyers to target rich defendants.

   The proportionate liability of proportionately liable defendants can exceed their percentage of responsibility in two respects. First, if the liability share of any codefendant is found to be uncollectible within six months of entry of the judgment, proportionately liable defendants will be liable for the uncollectible portion in proportion to their share of responsibility, up to 50 % of each covered person's proportionate share. Second, plaintiffs with net worth of under $200,000 and who incur damages equal to more than 10% of their net worth could still enforce their judgment against all defendants jointly and severally.

   The Act also clarifies a number of open issues concerning the operation of rights of contribution among codefendants. A defendant who settles a private action is discharged from all claims of contribution brought by other persons, and any subsequent judgment in the action is reduced by the greater of the percentage of responsibility of the settling defendant or the amount paid to the plaintiff by the settling defendant. A defendant against whom a judgment is not collectible is subject to contribution and to continuing liability to the plaintiff. A proportionate share of responsibility has a contribution claim against other defendants, except settling defendants, or any other person responsible for the conduct. All claims for contribution are to be determined based on the percentage of responsibility of the claimant and of each person who would have been liable if joined in the original action. Contribution claims are subject to a six-month statute of limitations.

2) A significant part of the Act for the various professions is its system of proportionate liability which the professions had urged Congress to adopt as part of the legislation. For example, a defendant who is found only to have acted carelessly, and did not *knowingly* commit fraud,

would be responsible for a proportionate amount of the damages instead of for the fullest amount of money possible as under the old law.

3) All defendants involved in the action remain jointly and severally liable to investors with a net worth under $200,000 who lost more than 10% of their net worth. Defendants liable for their proportionate share are also liable for up to an additional 50% of their share to help pay for insolvent codefendants.

4) The Act encourages voluntary disclosure of forward-looking information to investors by establishing a carefully designed safe harbor rule. The safe harbor protects statements made and meaningful cautionary risk disclosures that identify factors that could alter actual results.

5) Language was added to the safe harbor provision to make certain that forward-looking information has meaningful support behind it. The safe harbor does not protect those who knowingly make a false or misleading statement.

6) The 1995 Act requires that auditors immediately disclose illegal acts discovered in the course of an audit. Auditors must notify the SEC of illegal acts ignored or improperly considered by management. This puts a time limit on when illegal acts must be reported to the SEC. The board of directors has *one* business day to report to the SEC that the independent auditor has reported a material illegal act, and the auditor has determined that senior management and the board of directors have not taken appropriate actions, or are not expected to take appropriate action. If the independent auditor does not receive a copy of the board of directors' report to the SEC within the one business day period, the independent auditor must resign from the engagement or furnish the SEC with a copy of the original fraud report. This requirement ensures immediate reporting of illegal acts.

7) The Act gives the SEC the power to sue people or companies for aiding and abetting others who commit fraud. The provision is designed to ensure the SEC's enforcement authority which prevents aiding and abetting from not being considered an actionable offense in private securities fraud lawsuits.

8) The law does not require the loser of a case to pay all attorneys' fees, but it does impose sanctions against attorneys who file frivolous lawsuits. If a court finds that either the plaintiff's or the defendant's attorneys made arguments that were legally irrelevant or lacking evidentiary support, the court must impose sanctions unless it is a trifling violation. Reasonable attorneys' costs and fees are presumed to be adequate reimbursement. The statute of limitations is not changed with respect to the three-year time limit for filing securities fraud lawsuits. Current law permits actions to be brought within one year after discovery of an alleged violation, and no more than three years after the alleged violation occurred.

CERTIFICATION FILED WITH COMPLAINT

Each plaintiff seeking to serve as a representative party on behalf of a class must provide a sworn certification, which shall be personally signed by the plaintiff and filed with the complaint, that states that the plaintiff has reviewed the complaint and authorized this filing, and states that the plaintiff did not purchase the security that is the subject of the complaint at the direction of plaintiff's counsel or in order to participate in any private action.

NONWAIVER OF ATTORNEY PRIVILEGE

The certification filed shall not be construed to be a waiver of the attorney-client privilege.

APPOINTMENT OF LEAD PLAINTIFF

No later than 20 days after the date on which the complaint is filed, the plaintiff or plaintiffs shall cause to be published, in a widely circulated national business oriented publication or wire service, a notice advising members of the purported plaintiff class of the action, and the claims asserted therein. Not later than 60 days after the date on which the notice is published, any member of the purported class may move the court to serve as lead plaintiff of the purported class.

No later than 90 days after the date on which a notice is published, the court shall consider any motion made by a class member who is not individually named as a plaintiff in the complaint or complaints, and shall appoint as lead plaintiff the member or members of the purported plaintiff class that the court determines to be most capable of adequately representing the interests of class members who is referred to as the *most adequate plaintiff.*

ADDITIONAL NOTICES REQUIRED UNDER FEDERAL RULES

Notice required under the early notice requirement should be in addition to any other required notice.

CONSOLIDATED ACTIONS

If more than one action on behalf of a class asserts substantially the same claim or claims for pretrial purposes or trial, the court will appoint the most adequate plaintiff as lead plaintiff for the consolidated actions.

REBUTTABLE PRESUMPTION

The court shall adopt a presumption that the most adequate plaintiff in any private action is the person or group of persons who has either filed the complaint, or made a motion in response to a notice in the determination of the court, and has the largest financial interest in the relief sought by the class.

DISCOVERY

Discovery relating to whether a member or members of the purported plaintiff class is the most adequate plaintiff can be conducted by a plaintiff only if the plaintiff first demonstrates a reasonable basis for a finding that the presumptively most adequate plaintiff is incapable of adequately representing the class.

SELECTION OF LEAD COUNSEL

The most adequate plaintiff will, subject to the approval of the court, select and retain counsel to represent the class.

RESTRICTIONS ON PROFESSIONAL PLAINTIFFS

A person may be a lead plaintiff, or an officer, director, or fiduciary of a lead plaintiff, in no more than five securities class actions brought as plaintiff class actions.

RECOVERY BY PLAINTIFFS

The share of any final judgment or of any settlement that is awarded to a representative party serving on behalf of a class shall be equal, on a per share basis, to the portion of the final judgment or settlement awarded to all members of the class. However, the court may permit lead plaintiffs to recover reasonable costs and expenses, including lost wages.

RESTRICTIONS ON SETTLEMENTS UNDER SEAL

The terms and provisions of any settlement of a class action should not be filed under seal, except that on motion of any party to the settlement, the court can order filing under seal for those portions of a settlement agreement as to which good cause is shown for a filing under seal.

Restrictions on Payment of Attorneys' Fees and Expenses

Total attorneys' fees and expenses awarded by the court to counsel for the plaintiff class shall not exceed a reasonable percentage of the amount of any damage and prejudgment interest actually paid to the class.

Disclosure of Settlement Terms to Class Members

Any proposed or final settlement agreement that is published or otherwise disseminated to the class will include a cover page summarizing the information contained in the following statements:

Statement of plaintiff recovery. The amount of the settlement proposed to be distributed to the parties to the action, is determined in the aggregate and on an average per share basis.

Agreement of the amount of damages. If the settling parties agree on the average amount of damages per share that would be recoverable if the plaintiff prevailed on each claim alleged, a statement concerning the average amount of such potential damages per share, and a statement from each settling party should be made.

Disagreement on the amount of damages. If the parties do not agree on the average amount of damages per share that would be recoverable if the plaintiff prevailed on each claim alleged, a statement from each settling party must be made concerning the issue or issues on which the parties disagree.

Inadmissibility for certain purposes. A statement made concerning the amount of damages shall not be admissible in any federal or state judicial action or administrative proceeding, other than an action or proceeding arising out of such statement.

Statement of attorneys' fees or costs sought. If any of the settling parties or their counsel intend to apply to the court for an award of attorneys' fees or costs from any fund established as part of the settlement, a statement indicating which parties or counsel intend to make such an application, the amount of such fees and costs determined on an average per share basis, and a brief explanation supporting the fees and costs sought is required. Such information will be clearly summarized on the cover page of any notice to a party of any proposed or final settlement agreement.

Identification of lawyers' representatives. The name, telephone number, and address of one or more representatives of counsel for the plaintiff class who will be reasonably available to answer questions from the class.

Reasons for settlement. A brief statement explaining the reasons why the parties are proposing the settlement must be made.

Other information. Information that might be required by the court.

ATTORNEY CONFLICT OF INTEREST

If a plaintiff class is represented by an attorney who directly owns or otherwise has a beneficial interest in the securities that are the subject of a litigation, the court shall make a determination of whether such ownership or other interest constitutes a conflict of interest sufficient to disqualify the attorney from representing the plaintiff class.

SECURITY FOR PAYMENT OF COSTS IN CLASS ACTIONS

In any private action that is certified as a class action, the court may require an undertaking from the attorneys for the plaintiff class, the plaintiffs' class, or both, in such proportions and at such times as the court determines are just and equitable for the payment of fees and expenses that may be awarded.

The Act does permit a court to require plaintiffs, defendants, or their attorneys to post a bond for the payment of fees and expenses that may be awarded.

MISLEADING STATEMENTS AND OMISSIONS

In actions in which the plaintiff alleges that the defendant made an untrue statement of a material fact, or omitted a material fact necessary to prevent the statements from being misleading, the complaint must specify the following:

1) Each statement alleged to have been misleading,
2) The reason or reasons why the statement is misleading, and
3) If an allegation regarding the statement or omission is made on information and belief, the complaint should state the specific facts on which that belief is based.

REQUIRED STATE OF MIND

In any private action in which the plaintiff may recover money damages only on proof that the defendant acted with a particular state of mind, the complaint shall state specifically which facts give rise to a strong inference that the defendant acted with the required state of mind.

SANCTION FOR WILLFUL VIOLATION

A party aggrieved by the willful failure of an opposing party to comply with this Act may apply to the court for an order awarding appropriate sanctions.

CAUSATION OF LOSS

In any private action, the plaintiff shall have the burden of proving that the act or omission of the defendant alleged to violate this Act caused the loss for which the plaintiff seeks to recover damages.

LIMITATION ON DAMAGES

Stock prices frequently have a tendency to recover part of their market price after the initial price adjustment to adverse news about a company. If a security recovers some or all of its market price during the 90-day period after the dissemination of information correcting the misstatement or omission that is the basis for the action, damages will be capped at the difference between the price paid for the security and the mean trading price of the security during the 90-day period.

If the plaintiff sells or repurchases the subject security prior to the expiration of the 90-day period, the plaintiff's damages shall not exceed the difference between the purchase or sale price paid or received, as appropriate, by the plaintiff for the security and the mean trading price of the security during the period beginning immediately after dissemination of information correcting the misstatement or omission and ending on the date on which the plaintiff sells or repurchases the security. For the purposes of this rule, the *mean trading price* of a security shall be an average of the daily trading price of that security, determined as of the close of the market each day during the 90-day period.

PRIVATE CLASS ACTIONS

The provisions of this Act shall apply in each private action arising that is brought as a plaintiff class action.

Multiple Actions

If more than one action is filed on behalf of a class asserting substantially the same claim or claims, only the plaintiff or plaintiffs in the first filed action will be required to cause notice to be published.

Presumption in Favor of Attorneys' Fees and Costs for Abusive Litigation

The court shall adopt a presumption that the appropriate sanction for failure of any responsive pleading, or dispositive motion to comply with any requirement of the court, is an award to the opposing party of the reasonable attorneys' fees and other expenses incurred as a direct violation.

Rebuttal Evidence for Sanctions Against Abusive Litigation

The presumption may be rebutted only upon proof by the party, or attorney against whom sanctions are to be imposed, that the award of attorneys' fees and other expenses will impose an unreasonable burden on that party or attorney and would be unjust, and the failure to make such an award would not impose a greater burden on the party in whose favor sanctions are to be imposed. If the party or attorney against whom sanctions are to be imposed meets its burden, the court shall award the sanctions that the court deems appropriate.

Availability of Documents

Any document filed with the Commission or generally disseminated shall be deemed to be readily available.

Stay Pending Decision on Motion Exemption Authority

In any private action, the court shall stay discovery, other than discovery that is specifically directed to the application of an exemption, during the tendency of any motion by a defendant for summary judgment that is based on the ground that the statement or omission upon which the complaint is used is a forward-looking statement, and the exemption provided precludes a claim for relief.

EXEMPTION AUTHORITY

The Commission may provide presumptions from any provision of this Act that is consistent with the public interest and the protection of investors as determined by the Commission.

EFFECT ON OTHER AUTHORITY OF THE COMMISSION

Nothing in the Act limits, either expressly or by implication, the authority of the Commission to exercise similar authority or to adopt similar rules and regulations with respect to forward-looking statements under any other statute under which the Commission exercises rule-making authority.

DEFINITION OF FORWARD-LOOKING STATEMENTS

Forward-Looking Statement. The term means a statement containing a projection of revenues, income including income loss, earnings including earnings loss per share, capital expenditures, dividends, capital structure, or other financial items. These could include, but are not limited to, the following:

- A statement of the plans and objectives of management for future operations, including plans or objectives relating to the products or services of the issuer.
- A statement of future economic performance, including any such statement contained in a discussion and analysis of financial condition by the management or in results of operations included pursuant to the rules and regulations of the Commission.
- Any statement of the admissions underlying or relating to any other statement.
- Any report issued by an outside reviewer retained by an issuer, to the extent that the report assesses a forward-looking statement made by the issuer.
- A statement containing a projection or estimate of such other items as may be specified by rule or regulation of the Commission.

SAFE HARBOR FOR FORWARD-LOOKING STATEMENTS

Liability for forward-looking statements such as earnings or sales forecasts has had the undesirable effect of discouraging companies from sharing such information with investors, despite keen market interest in this information. This has become a particular concern for high technology companies which tend to have volatile stock prices, and therefore are frequent targets of class action lawsuits when projections are not realized. While the primary beneficiaries of the safe harbor are issuers and their officers, the Act also offers useful protection to broker-dealers in their roles as underwriters and analysts. The safe harbor is offered to:

1) An issuer who, at the time that the statement is made, is subject to the reporting requirements of the Exchange Act.
2) A person acting on behalf of such issuer.
3) An outside reviewer retained by such issuer making a statement on behalf of such issuer.
4) An underwriter, with respect to information provided by such issuer or information derived from information provided by the issuer.

In addition, the safe harbor excludes certain categories of issuers and transactions, most notably issuers who have been subject to criminal or SEC enforcement sanctions within the preceding three years, issuers that are investment companies, and statements made in connection with a tender offer or initial public offering, or that are included in an audited financial statement. The safe harbor generally applies to a forward-looking statement if it is identified as a forward-looking statement, and is accompanied by meaningful cautionary statements identifying important factors that could cause actual results to differ materially from those in the forward-looking statement; or is immaterial; or the plaintiff fails to prove the forward-looking statement was made with actual knowledge; or if made by a business entity was made by and with the approval of an executive officer of that entity, and made or approved by such officer with actual knowledge by that officer that the statement was false or misleading.

Oral statements made by an issuer, or by a person acting on behalf of such issuer, can also be covered under a corollary formulation of the safe harbor. Under the corollary, an oral statement qualifies for the safe harbor if the oral statement is accompanied by a cautionary statement pointing out that the oral statement is a forward-looking statement that actual results may vary, and identifying an available written document setting out the meaningful cautionary statements identifying important factors that could cause actual results to differ that are required by the primary safe harbor.

The safe harbor was drafted in such a way that even if a forward-looking projection or estimate did not contain adequate cautionary language, a plaintiff would still have to prove that the speaker had actual knowledge that the statement was false or misleading. The safe harbor directs courts to stay all discovery, except for discovery directed at the applicability of the safe harbor, while a motion to dismiss based on the safe harbor is pending.

CLASS ACTION REFORMS

The Act creates a procedure for the court to appoint as lead plaintiff the plaintiff with the largest financial interest. The Act also adopts other class action reforms, such as prohibiting the payment of referral fees to securities brokers.

PROPORTIONATE LIABILITY AND CONTRIBUTIONS

The Act generally limits joint and several liability to persons who knowingly commit a violation of the securities laws. The Act requires a defendant to pay 50% more than its proportionate share of damages in certain cases where other defendants' shares are uncollectible, and preserves joint and several liability for plaintiffs with a net worth under $200,000 whose damages exceed 10% of their net worth. The Act clarifies certain issues regarding the operation of rights of contribution.

REDUCTION OF DAMAGE

The Act provides that a defendant can reduce damages by proving that all or part of the decline in the value of the securities was caused by factors other than the alleged misstatement or material omission in the prospectus.

RIGHT OF RESCISSION

The Act provides a right of rescission to the buyer of a security if the security was sold in violation of the registration or prospectus delivery requirements, or if it was offered or sold by means of a prospectus or oral communication which included an untrue statement of a material fact or omitted to state a material fact.

AIDING AND ABETTING

The Act gives the SEC (but not private plaintiffs) authority to bring civil injunctive actions and to seek civil money penalties against any person who knowingly provides substantial assistance to another person in violation of the Exchange Act to the same extent as the person to whom such assistance is provided.

Stay of Discovery and Preservation of Evidence

A stay of discovery is required while a motion to dismiss is pending, other than a particular discovery needed to preserve evidence. Any party to the action with actual notice of the allegations contained in the complaint shall treat all documents, data compilation, and tangible objects that are in the custody or control of such person and that are relevant to the allegations, as if they were the subject of a continuing request for production of documents from an opposing party. A party aggrieved by the willful failure of an opposing party to comply with this requirement may apply to the court for sanctions. The use of the term *willful failure* should give protection from liability for inadvertent violations.

Protections for Senior Citizens and Qualified Investment Retirement Plans

The SEC must determine whether senior citizens or qualified retirement plans have been adversely impacted by abusive securities fraud litigation and whether they are adequately protected from such litigation by the Act. If the SEC finds any such adverse impact or lack of adequate protection, it is to submit to Congress a report containing recommendations for protection from securities fraud, or for protection from abusive litigation.

Racketeer Influenced and Corrupt Organization Act (RICO)

The Act eliminates private RICO liability, with its accompanying exposure to treble damages, for conduct that would have been actionable as fraud in the purchase or sale of securities. This does not apply to an action against any person who is criminally convicted in connection with the fraud, in which case the statute of limitations will begin to run from the date the conviction becomes final.

Proportionate Liability

Major accounting firms argued that joint and several liability under the antifraud provisions of the securities laws had created an unjustifiable liability exposure in cases where their role was relatively peripheral, but their potential deep-pocket liability for the more culpable conduct of others was enormous. Accounting firms argued that this disproportionate liability exposure was forcing them to curtail audit services for companies that were regarded as high risks for potential litigation; particularly start-up firms and firms with volatile stock prices in the high technology sectors. In place of joint and several liability, accounting firms sought a limited system of proportionate liability, so that the liability of less culpable defendants would bear some relationship to their degree of responsibility for the damages incurred.

The Act provides that a defendant in an action is jointly and severally liable only if the person who tries the facts specifically finds that the defendant *knowingly committed* a violation of the securities laws. The provision provides an extensive clarification of the term, which essentially requires that the defendant engaged in conduct with actual knowledge of the facts and circumstances that make the conduct a violation of the securities laws. The Act also expressly provides that *reckless conduct* will not be construed to constitute a knowing commission of a violation of the securities laws. The Act also takes pains to avoid supporting the argument that recklessness is a sufficient standard for anti-fraud liability by providing that nothing in the Act should be construed to create, affect, or in any manner modify, the standard of liability associated with any action arising under the securities laws. For defendants who are not found to have committed a knowing violation of the securities laws, the Act offers a qualified form of proportionate liability. Such a defendant is only liable for the portion of the judgment that corresponds to its percentage of responsibility. In determining the percentage of responsibility for each defendant, the person examining the facts must consider:

1) The nature of the conduct of each covered person found to have caused or contributed to the loss incurred by the plaintiff or plaintiffs.

2) The nature and extent of the causal relationship between the conduct of each such person and the damages incurred by the plaintiff or plaintiffs.

INDEMNIFICATION AGREEMENTS

The indemnification agreement expressly permits a defendant to recover attorney's fees and costs incurred in connection with an action in which the defendant prevails. The Act does not change the enforceability of indemnification contracts in the event of settlement.

RULE OF CONSTRUCTION

The Act clarifies two points:

1) Nothing in the Act is to be deemed to prevent the SEC from restricting or otherwise regulating private actions under the Exchange Act.

2) Nothing in the Act is to be deemed to create or ratify any implied right of action.

The Act's Exception Provision

The Act's exception for material of little value could alleviate a concern about the Act's use of the term *substantial* in relation to complaints. The word *substantial* might be used to argue that plaintiffs' complaints are to be subjected to a less rigorous scrutiny than papers filed by other parties. The ability to rebut any finding of a violation by showing that the finding was of little value suggests that the standard probably will be the same for both plaintiffs and defendants. Although it is not clear whether there is some distinction intended between substantial and irrelevancy, *the exception provision* in the Act was not the intention of Congress to hold defendants to a more stringent standard than plaintiffs.

Conclusion

The Act reforms many of the procedures that govern private class actions. It is intended to address a number of concerns about securities class actions, such as the race to the courthouse to file cases within days or even hours of a sharp stock price decline; the ability of attorneys to select plaintiffs with nominal holdings to bring a class action case; the lack of opportunities for institutional investors to participate in litigation brought on their behalf; and the lack of effective notice to investors of the terms of class action settlements. Institutional investors are encouraged to take a more active role in securities class action lawsuits. Within 20 days of filing a class action lawsuit, the plaintiff must provide notice to members of the purported class. The notice is to identify the claims alleged in the lawsuit and indicate that potential members have 60 days from publication to file a motion to seek to serve as lead plaintiff. If more than one action is filed, only the plaintiff in the first action is required to file the notice. The notice must be filed in a widely circulated business publication.

Once designated by the court, the lead plaintiff is authorized to select and retain counsel for the class. It is unclear whether this provision would encompass other related powers, such as to replace counsel, to direct litigation strategy, or to reject or give preliminary approval to settlements. The amount of autonomy that courts actually give to lead plaintiffs to manage the case could have a significant impact on whether institutional investors will avail themselves of this new procedure.

Chapter 12

The Securities and Exchange Commission: Disclosure Simplification

The Securities and Exchange Commission's Task Force on Disclosure Simplification released the results of their study and the proposals for implementing their findings in March, 1996. Their assignment was to "review rules and forms affecting capital formation, with a view toward streamlining, simplifying, and modernizing the overall regulatory scheme without compromising or diminishing important investor protection."

During their study, the members reviewed forms and rules relating to capital-raising transactions; periodic reporting in conformance with the Exchange Act; and proxy solicitations, tender offers, and beneficial ownership reports under the Williams Act. Suggestions were sought and received from interested organizations and hundreds of suggestions and recommendations were taken into consideration.

As might be expected, along with suggestions for handling corporate finance were also recommendations on accounting disclosure changes. In formulating its recommendations concerning these potential changes, the Task Force received suggestions from a number of participants in the financial reporting process. Many of the Task Force's recommendations that are discussed below reflect the input received from these participants.

However, members of the group felt that other suggestions for accounting disclosure changes were important and required further study and consideration. As a part of a longer-term review, the following will be studied:

1) Integration of the financial reporting requirements of Regulation S-X with the narrative disclosure requirements of Regulation S-K in one comprehensive package.

2) Modification of the interim reporting scheme.

The longer-range project is also needed to evaluate the recommendations of the various private sector organizations that have issued reports on the information needs of users of financial information. Those reports make a number of recommendations to enhance the utility of financial reporting that will be considered by accounting standard setters, particularly the Financial Accounting Standards Board (FASB), and by regulators, such as the SEC.

There were five areas in general in which the Task Force was prepared to make recommendations and suggestions for accounting disclosure changes.

INCOME AVERAGING

The first of these would permit companies to *income average* when determining the significance of acquisitions and equity method investments, thereby refining the circumstances when the company must provide separate financial statements to those instances where the acquisition or investment is truly significant.

In addition to their own financial statements, registrants are often required to present separate audited financial statements of other persons in filings with the Commission. The two most common situations where separate audited financial statements of another person are required in registrant's filings relate to:

1) Business acquisitions where the acquired business exceeds 10% in significance.

2) Financial statements of equity method investees when the significance of the investee to the registrant exceeds 20%.

Significance is measured using the three significant subsidiary tests of the appropriate rule of Regulation S-X, one of which is a comparison of the investee's income to the registrant's income.

Under current rules, if the registrant's income for the most recent fiscal year is 10% or more lower than the average of the last five fiscal years, the registrant may elect to use the average income for purposes of determining significance under the significant subsidiary tests, thereby reducing the level of significance of the investee and eliminating or reducing the requirements to present its audited financial statements.

However, the rule allowing registrants to income average is not applicable if the registrant reported a loss, rather than income, in the latest fiscal year. In such circumstances, the test could operate to require unnecessary disclosure, particularly with respect to companies with relatively small losses in the latest fiscal year.

The Task Force proposes changing the rules to allow registrants to income average, for purposes of determining significance, whenever the registrant's income or loss for the most recent fiscal year is 10% or more lower than the average of the last five fiscal years.

Implementation of this recommendation would require a revision to the definition of *significant subsidiary* in Regulation S-X.

MODIFICATION OF THE BLACKOUT

The second of these would be to reduce the effect of the 45-day *blackout* period during which many registrants are effectively prevented from undertaking a public offering by narrowing the scope of the accounting rules requiring updated audited financial statements in certain registration statements declared effective 45 days after the registrant's fiscal year-end.

The Exchange Act generally requires filing of audited annual financial statements of a registrant 90 days after the end of the registrant's most recently completed fiscal year. However, unless the registrant meets the requirements of Regulation S-X relating to expected profits for the most recent fiscal year and a history of profitable operations, registration statements filed under the Securities Act must include audited financial statements of the registrant for the registrant's most recent fiscal year if the registrant statement is declared effective more than 45 days after the registrant's fiscal year.

This requirement to provide updated audited financial statements 45 days after a registrant's fiscal year is difficult for many registrants to satisfy, and in some circumstances, prevents a registrant from filing a Securities Act registration statement during this 45-day blackout period.

The Task Force believes that the requirement to provide updated audited financial statements in Securities Act filings sooner than required under the Exchange Act should be eliminated for repeat issuers.

This recommendation would not alter current requirements relating to initial public offerings under the Securities Act.

MODIFICATION OF FILINGS FOR SIGNIFICANT INVESTEES

The Task Force is proposing to expand the circumstances in which a company may incorporate by reference audited financial statements of *significant investees* so that such statements need not be reproduced in filings with the Commission.

Following requirements in Regulation S-X, registrants are required to provide audited financial statements of *significant investees* accounted for under the equity method. An investee is *significant* if the registrant's investment exceeds 20% of the registrant's total assets or the investee provides more than 20% of the registrant's income.

The Task Force recommends clarifying current rules to state more explicitly that registrants may incorporate such financial statements by reference in all reports and filings under the Exchange Act, and, consequently, that registrant's filing on Forms S-3 or F-3 may incorporate by reference their Exchange Act reports containing such financial information.

The Task Force also recommends permitting issuers eligible to use Forms S-1 or F-1 that have been reporting for 12 months to deliver the financial statements of *significant investees* in lieu of restating them in the prospectus, and to incorporate by reference financial statements of *significant investees* who are eligible to use Forms S-3 or F-3.

They also believe that the SEC should consider whether such relief should be extended to all classes of issuers.

SIMPLIFICATION OF RULES RELATING TO AFFILIATES AND GUARANTORS

The Task Force is also recommending that the SEC should streamline the complex and often confusing rules requiring separate audited financial statements of affiliates whose stock collateralizes a registrant's securities, and of persons who guarantee a registrant's securities.

Regulation S-X requires separate audited financial statements of each affiliate whose stock constitutes a significant portion of the collateral for any public issuance of the registrant's securities. In addition, it requires a registrant to file separate audited financial statements of each guarantor of the registrant's publicly issued securities.

As currently written and interpreted by the staff, this specific requirement can lead to multiple sets of financial statements even though in many instances such financial statements may be of limited usefulness to investors. The Task Force believes that simplification and streamlining of this rule are necessary.

The following recommendations have been divided into two separate sections, the first dealing with collateralizations and the second dealing with guarantees.

1) Financial statements of affiliates whose stock collateralizes securities of a registrant: Rule 3-10 currently provides that the collateral is significant, and thus audited financial statements of the affiliate whose stock constitutes the collateral are required when the book value, fair value or market value of the collateral exceeds 20% of the principal amount of the secured class of securities.

   The Task Force recommends that audited financial statements of the affiliate should be required only when the value of the securities of the affiliate which collateralize the securities of the registrant exceeds 40% of the principal amount of the secured class of securities.

If the value of the collateral constitutes between 20% and 40% of the principal amount of the secured class of securities, the Task Force recommends the rules be revised to require only condensed financial statements of the affiliate. Such condensed financial information could be placed in an audited footnote to the registrant's financial statements, provided, however, the affiliate is consolidated with the registrant.

2) Financial statements of guarantor: The rules requiring separate financial statements of each guarantor of a security are currently contained in Staff Accounting Bulletin (SAB) 53 and Rule 3-10 of Regulation S-X, as interpreted through various no-action positions taken by the Division staff. In addition, the guarantor, if a subsidiary of the issuer, or the issuer, if the issuer is a subsidiary of the guarantor, must file periodic reports under the Exchange Act unless it obtains special reporting relief. This relief normally is granted only if the guarantor or the issuer is wholly owned and the guarantee is full and unconditional.

The current financial statement requirements for guarantors are complex, provide for multiple outcomes, depending on the corporate structure of the registrant and the level of significance of any nonguaranteeing subsidiaries, and, furthermore, are not understood by many registrants.

The Task Force recommends that the Commission simplify the reporting alternatives under Rule 3-10 and SAB 53, and clarify the definition of *wholly-owned subsidiary* to be consistent with the definition in the general instructions in Form 10-K. The Task Force further recommends that, if the guarantee is full, unconditional and joint and several, the SEC require either summarized consolidating financial information or condensed consolidating financial statements, depending upon the significance of any nonguaranteeing subsidiaries. This would greatly simplify the process and actually provide more useful information to investors than is currently provided in many circumstances.

If only summarized consolidating financial information is required, it should be on the condition that in the event of a default on the security or other events which increase the need for disclosure of information relating to the issuer or guarantor, the level of disclosure increases and condensed consolidation financial information or full financial statements would be required. If the guarantees are not full, unconditional and joint and several, or the affiliate is wholly-owned, separate audited financial statements would continue to be required.

ELIMINATION AND MODIFICATION OF DUPLICATIVE AND OBSOLETE ACCOUNTING ITEMS

The last of these recommendations would streamline accounting and related disclosure requirements by eliminating duplicative rules and those rules that have outlived their usefulness.

The accounting and related disclosures required in SEC documents are governed by GAAP and the rules and regulations of the Commission. GAAP applies to all companies, while the rules and regulations of the Commission apply primarily to public companies.

Therefore, when preparing Commission documents, registrants must comply with GAAP as well as Commission accounting rules, most of which are contained in Regulation S-X. In many cases, the Commission adopted rules that were subsequently codified by the Financial Accounting Standards Board (FASB) as a part of GAAP. In addition, when more than one independent body is making rules for disclosure for different but overlapping populations, it is inevitable that some duplication will occur. As a result, over the years, redundancies have developed between the FASB accounting rules and Regulation S-X.

NOTE: The items listed below become very specific, technical, and rather inclusive; however, they do give a good indication of the Task Force's serious intent to attempt a simplification of the filing process.

The recommended changes made to the accounting items listed below are intended to eliminate SEC accounting rules where information required under a rule basically duplicates information required by other current accounting regulations, or where the accounting rule has simply outlived its usefulness.

1) Eliminate Rule 3-12 of Regulation S-X, which sets forth the requirements regarding the age of financial statements at the effective date of a registration statement or at the mailing of a proxy statement. Since this rule largely duplicates the information contained in Rules 3-01 and 3-02, the Task Force recommended its elimination and the merging of any non-duplicative portions into Rules 3-01 and 3-02.

2) Eliminate subparagraph (a) of Rule 3-15 of Regulation S-X, which relates to the format of the income statement and balance sheet of real estate investment trusts (REITs). GAAP adequately provides for the formatting of the balance sheets and income statements for REITs.

3) Eliminate Rule 3-16 of Regulation S-X, which sets forth the requirements for registrants that have emerged from a corporate reorganization. The disclosures required by GAAP (including SOP 90-7, "Reorganizations Under the Bankruptcy Code") and Item 303 of Regulation S-K (Management's Discussion and Analysis) adequately cover this information.

4) Eliminate Rule 4-05 of Regulation S-X, which relates to current assets and current liabilities when a company's operating cycle is longer than one year. Current GAAP disclosures are adequate.

5) Eliminate Rule 4-06 of Regulation S-X, which states that reacquired indebtedness of a registrant must be deducted from the appropriate lia-

bility caption on the registrant's balance sheet. GAAP and current accounting practices require this.

6) Eliminate Rule 4-07 of Regulation S-X, which relates to the mandated balance sheet presentation for discounts on shares. It is outdated and unnecessary.

7) Eliminate subparagraphs (f) and (k)(1) and modify subparagraph (m) of Rule 4-08 of Regulation S-X. Rule 4-08 relates to the general notes to the financial statements. Subparagraph (f), relating to significant changes in bonds, mortgages and similar debt, and subparagraph (k)(1), relating to related party disclosures, should be deleted from Rule 4-08 because disclosure under current GAAP, including FASB 57, appears to be adequate.

Subparagraph (m), relating to repurchase agreements, should be revised to eliminate the disclosure requirements already required by FASB 107 and FASB 115.

8) Eliminate subparagraphs (b) through (h) of Rule 4-10 of Regulation S-X, which set forth the requirements under the successful efforts accounting method followed by oil and gas producers. This duplicates requirements of FASB 19.

Specific rules for both the successful efforts and full cost accounting methods were maintained in Regulation S-X as a result of the SEC's action to supersede the FASB's determination to designate successful efforts as the method of accounting to be applied uniformly by all oil and gas producers.

9) Eliminate or modify Article 7 of Regulation S-X, which relates to requirements for insurance companies. It could be eliminated because the AICPA Industry Guides adequately cover disclosures by insurance companies.

However, if Article 7 is deleted, the provisions of Notes 6 to 7-03(a), relating to disclosure of investments in excess of 10% of shareholders' equity, should be incorporated into Industry Guide 6 (Property Casualty Insurance Claims).

Alternatively, Rule 7-02(b) could be eliminated because its requirements are covered by FASB 120 and SOP 95-1.

Any change to Article 7 would require corresponding changes to the EDGAR Financial Data Schedules, which are based in part on information elicited by disclosure requirements in Article 7.

10) Modify Rule 10-01(a) of Regulation S-X, which gives requirements for condensed financial statements to be filed for interim periods. In 1992, interim reporting requirements were modified for small businesses. In recommending this action, the staff highlighted its potential to be substituted for the current Rule 10-01(a). Rule 10-01(a) may now be rewritten to be consistent with the modifications adopted for small business issuers under Regulation S-B. This revision would reduce the degree of detail required and would make the small business modifications applicable to all registrants filing interim reports.

11) Eliminate Staff Accounting Bulletin 43. This bulletin provides guidance concerning the early adoption of new rules for separate financial statements required by Regulation S-X. Guidance is no longer necessary due to lapse of time.

12) Eliminate or Modify Staff Accounting Bulletin 50. The Task Force recommended that general instruction G to Form S-4, relating to the filing and effectiveness of registration statements involving the formation of bank holding companies, and requests for confidential treatment be eliminated. If this instruction is eliminated, the Commission should consider eliminating or modifying SAB 50, which relates to financial statement requirements in filings involving the formation of a bank holding company.

13) Modify Staff Accounting Bulletin 80, which provides guidance relating to the application of Rule 3-05 in initial public offerings. The Task Force recommends that this bulletin be revised to codify previous staff relief granted.

14) Eliminate Staff Accounting Bulletin 86, which provides guidance on accounting for the tax benefits of net operating loss carryforwards that existed as of the date of a quasi reorganization. The guidance is based on FASB 96, which was amended by FASB 109. Eliminating SAB 86 would have the effect of deleting questions 4 and 5 from SAB Topic 5.S. SAB 86 may be eliminated because FASB 109 contains adequate guidance with respect to the accounting covered by those questions.

15) Eliminate Staff Accounting Bulletin 91, which provides guidance on accounting for income tax benefits of bad debts of thrifts. This guidance is unnecessary because of the issuance of FASB 109.

16) Eliminate Staff Accounting Bulletin Topic 12.A.4 This bulletin, which provides guidance in filings by Canadian registrants, is no longer necessary.

17) Eliminate Staff Accounting Bulletin Topic 5.C. This Bulletin provides guidance on accounting for tax benefits of loss carryforwards and is no longer necessary because of the issuance of FASB 109.

18) The Task Force feels that the Commission should consider eliminating or modifying Rule 3A-02 of Regulation S-X, Staff Accounting Bulletin 51, and Staff Accounting Bulletin 84 if, as expected, the FASB issues new standard on consolidation.

The FASB has issued an exposure draft of a proposed accounting standard to specify when entities should be included in consolidated financial statements. The comment period expired on January 15, 1996.

If the FASB issues new standards on consolidation, Rule 3A-02 of Regulation S-X, SAB 51, and SAB 84 should be reviewed to determine whether they duplicate FASB standards and should be deleted or modified.

19) Rescission of Staff Accounting Bulletin 57, which provided guidance relating to the accounting for stock warrants when issuance is contingent on achievement of certain future events. FASB Statement 123, *Accounting for Stock-Based Compensation* includes specific provisions for transactions with nonemployees that were effective as of December 15, 1995. Since transactions with nonemployees were the transactions that had been covered by SAB 57, the SAB was rescinded as of that date.

Chapter 13

Recommendations for Reducing the Costs of Securities Registration: Shelf Registration

DELAYED OFFERINGS AND SIMPLIFIED REPORTING BY SMALLER COMPANIES

Over a decade ago, the SEC significantly streamlined the registration process for certain large publicly traded issuers with three years of reporting history with the Commission. By introducing *shelf registration* for primary offerings of securities by these issuers, the Commission permitted certain relatively large, seasoned companies to sell some or all of the securities under an already effective registration statement at a time of their own choosing. In 1992, the Commission reduced the reporting period and market float requirements of Form S-3 to extend the benefits of shelf registration to a wider variety of issuers. This flexibility allowed such companies to take advantage of perceived *market windows.*

The Task Force is recommending now that a modified shelf registration procedure be provided to smaller companies that have filed timely public reports with the Commission for at least 12 months. This would provide approximately 4,800 companies with greater flexibility with respect to the timing of their offerings.

The Task Force also recommends permitting these smaller companies to deliver certain prior periodic reports to prospective investors instead of repeating similar information in the prospectus. This method, now used by companies filing on Forms S-2 or F-2 and reporting for 36 months, saves printing and other costs and results in a streamlined registration statement more focused on the proposed transaction. The Task Force believes that this method should be expanded to issuers who have been timely reporting for at least 12 months and using Forms S-1 or F-1. This would make Forms S-2 or F-2 superfluous.

SHELF OFFERINGS

The Task Force recommended several revisions to the shelf registration procedure to provide increased flexibility to a wider array of companies with respect to their capital-raising activities. Among other things, these recommendations included

1) Permitting delayed pricing for registrants that have been reporting for 12 months.
2) Eliminating restrictions on *at-the-market offerings* by seasoned Form S-3 or F-3 eligible companies.
3) Permitting a modified universal registrant procedure.
4) Permitting short form universal shelf registration statements to include secondary resales.

SMALLER ISSUERS

One of the recommendations is that the SEC allow smaller companies to price the securities on a delayed basis in order to time securities offerings more effectively with opportunities in the marketplace. These smaller companies may not now be able to take advantage of market windows for their securities because they are not eligible to use the Commission's shelf registration process for primary delayed offerings. The Task Force believes that the SEC should consider providing a modified form of shelf registration procedure to them.

The Task Force suggests that a procedure similar to existing ones, but without the requirement that a prospectus supplement containing pricing information be filed within 15 business days after the effective date of a registration statement, be provided to 12-month reporting companies. No changes to either the short form registration eligibility requirements or disclosure requirements are suggested. In short, the prospectus would be complete except with respect to pricing information permitted to be omitted under certain conditions. However, given that disclosure of certain terms of preferred or debt securities may not be practicable until pricing, they feel that the Commission should consider whether some additional flexibility with respect to delayed disclosure is appropriate for such securities. The Task Force contemplates that, like under existing rules, the pricing-related information contained in the pricing supplement would be deemed part of the registration statement, and accordingly this recommendation would not change the protections afforded investors under the liability provisions of the Securities Act.

As a result of this recommendation, approximately 4,800 smaller companies would be able to sell their securities on a delayed and continuous basis, as long as they deliver a pricing supplement containing the required information, their base prospectus, and any updating prospectus supplements. It has been suggested that providing additional flexibility to smaller companies could result in such entities raising more capital through the public markets rather than through exempt offerings conducted in the domestic and offshore markets.

While this recommendation would provide small companies time and cost savings, the Task Force is aware of concerns about possible adverse effects shelf registration could have in several instances:

1) The adequacy and accuracy of disclosures provided to investors.
2) On SEC oversight of the disclosures.
3) On the role of underwriters in the registration process.

These concerns are similar to those raised when the shelf registration rule was first being considered on a temporary basis in the early 1980s, and was made available to any offering including an initial public offering. One suggestion to address these concerns is to require a waiting period between the company's decision to sell its securities and the beginning of the offering. They suggest that during that period an underwriter could conduct a due diligence examination. Certain types of offerings, such as blind pools, penny stocks, and direct participation investment programs, have previously given rise to disclosure abuses. As a precaution against a problem along this line, the Task Force suggests formulating a modified shelf rule for smaller issuers using Form S-1, excluding, in whole or in part, such offerings from the procedure. Moreover, the Task Force anticipates that the registration statement and any post-effective amendment to reflect a fundamental change or to update the financial statements and other information in accordance with the Securities Act, as well as the company's periodic reports filed under the Exchange Act, would remain subject to Commission overseeing through the selective review process.

SEASONED ISSUERS

Another of the group's recommendations is that the SEC reconsider restrictions on at-the-market shelf offerings registered by seasoned issuers on Form S-3 or F-3.

An *at-the-market offering* is an offering on a national securities exchange or through a market-maker of securities for which there is an existing trading market. The Task Force suggests that the Commission reconsider the feasibility, consistent with investor protection and orderly market concerns, of eliminating one or more of the current restrictions on an at-the-market shelf offering to make it a more useful tool for capital-raising by seasoned issuers eligible to use Forms S-3 or F-3 for offerings of common stock and noninvestment grade securities.

Under current rules, a registrant may not make an at-the-market offering on Forms S-3 or F-3 unless certain conditions are met. The conditions are that:

1) The amount of securities registered cannot exceed 10% of the registrant's nonaffiliate public float; i.e., the aggregate market value of the registrant's outstanding voting stock held by nonaffiliates of the registrant.

2) The securities must be sold through an underwriter or underwriters acting as principal(s) or agent(s) for the registrant.

3) The underwriter or underwriters must be named in the prospectus.

Concerns have been raised as to whether elimination of any or all of the at-the-market offering requirements may have the unintended effect of impairing investor protection and contributing to disorderly markets. These concerns are similar to concerns raised when at-the-market offerings were initially considered by the Commission at the time that it adopted procedures for primary shelf registration. The Task Force therefore believes that further analysis of the use of at-the-market offerings, and reconsideration of those original concerns prompting inclusion of the restrictions on their use, particularly in light of subsequent regulatory changes, is necessary. This review should take into account the SEC's overall experience with the shelf registration process and subsequent regulatory changes, including the proposal of the Task Force to amend the trading practices rules.

INCLUSION OF SECONDARY OFFERINGS FOR SEASONED ISSUERS

After considering the general background of the shelf registration process, the Task Force is recommending that companies engaging in shelf offerings be permitted to include secondary offerings without identifying the selling security holders until the time of the actual offering.

In 1992, the Commission adopted provisions permitting universal shelf offerings in an effort to facilitate the use of shelf registration for delayed offerings of common stock and convertible securities. Universal shelf provisions permit registration of a dollar amount of securities without identifying the precise timing of each subsequent offering or specific amount of each class to be offered, provided the aggregate dollar amount of the securities to be offered is set forth in the registration statement. For example, a company can register an aggregate dollar amount, identify the classes of securities covered, and not allocate the specific amounts to be offered in each category. At the time of its adoption, the Commission only contemplated use of the universal shelf for primary offerings of securities. The Task Force does not believe that there is a need to retain that restriction and recommends that the Commission consider expansion of the universal shelf provisions to permit registration of secondary offerings. Under this proposal, issuers would not be required to identify the selling security holders until the time of the actual offering unless such identities are known prior to the date that the initial registration statement is declared effective.

Universal Registrant Rule

Additionally, the group is recommending that the SEC adopt a universal registrant rule, which would permit a parent company to name itself and its majority-owned subsidiaries as possible issuers on a shelf registration statement, and defer the choice of the actual issuer until the time of takedown.

In some instances, an issuer is not in a position to determine whether it or one of its subsidiaries will be issuing securities included on a shelf registration statement. The Commission staff has taken a no-action position where a registrant named itself as well as its wholly owned finance subsidiaries in a registration statement as possible issuers, so that the actual "issuer" could be chosen later at the time of the takedown.

They are recommending that the Commission consider the need for a rule that would more broadly permit an issuer to name on a registration statement itself and one or more of its majority-owned subsidiaries as possible issuers. This modification would eliminate pressure on multiple registrants to select prematurely the registrant, whether or not a finance or operating entity, who will be implementing the takedown from the shelf without reducing the level of significant information provided to investors.

Each registrant, however, would have to meet the eligibility requirements independently. Further, the financial and narrative disclosures in the registration statement would have to be complete with respect to each of the named registrants. Depending on the structure of the offering, a separate core registration statement may be required for each registrant. In addition, care would need to be taken to avoid the potential for investor confusion with respect to the issuer of the securities.

Post-Effective Amendment

The Task Force believes it would be useful to permit a company to reallocate securities, or register a new class of securities, on a shelf registration statement by post-effective amendment.

Present regulations require that a registrant file a new registration statement in order to supplement its offering with additional securities. However, the Task Force believes that the Commission should consider whether existing rules should be construed to preclude an issuer from either adding an additional class of securities or reallocating the securities registered on its registration statement by way of a post-effective amendment.

For example, a registrant originally registers one million dollars consisting of 100,000 shares of common stock priced at $5 per share and 100,000 shares of preferred stock also priced at $5 per share. If, some time after the registration statement is declared effective, the registrant decides to reallocate its one-million-dollar offering to include 50,000 shares of common stock and 150,000 shares of preferred stock, the registrant could do so by way of a post-effective amendment as long as the one-million-dollar offering amount is not exceeded.

Similarly, a company that has an effective one-million-dollar universal shelf registration statement covering senior securities may add common stock by means of a post-effective amendment as long as the one-million-dollar offering amount is not exceeded. If the one-million-dollar offering amount is exceeded under either example, the excess amount must be registered on a new registration statement, unless the recommendation described below, to permit registration of additional dollar amounts by post-effective amendment, is implemented by the Commission. Depending on the structure of the offering, this may require a separate core registration statement for each registrant.

The Task Force believes that the SEC should consider permitting seasoned issuers to register a dollar amount without specifying the classes of securities being registered.

Under current Commission rules, seasoned issuers are permitted to register dollar amounts of securities provided they identify the classes of securities covered by the registration statement for all securities they reasonably expect to issue over the ensuing two years. Since such issuers may not determine the specific terms of the securities until the actual offering date, disclosure regarding the classes of securities being registered is often general since most of the terms typically are not known at the effective date.

The Task Force recommends that the Commission consider the feasibility of allowing such seasoned issuers to register dollar amounts without specifying the classes of securities registered. Disclosure regarding the exact class and terms of securities to be offered would be provided at the time of the offering. As a result, such issuers would be afforded even greater flexibility in their capital-raising efforts than under the current regulations.

Furthermore, the Task Force recommends that such issuers be permitted to register additional dollar amounts by means of post-effective amendments rather than by the current procedure of filing a new registration statement.

REGISTRATION FEES AT TAKEDOWN

As a final measure to ease the financial pain of registration filings, the Task Force recommends allowing seasoned issuers to pay registration fees at the time securities are taken down from the shelf.

Although seasoned issuers may conduct delayed offerings by taking advantage of the shelf registration procedure, they are required to pay fees to the Commission upon the initial filing of the registration statement. As a result, issuers may be paying fees to the Commission months before they are actually offering securities to the public.

The Task Force suggests that the Commission consider its authority to implement a *pay-as-you-go* policy pursuant to which seasoned issuers would be permitted to pay fees at the time securities are taken down from the shelf. This would provide issuers with additional flexibility by allowing them the use of the funds required for Commission fees until the actual offering date.

Appendix A

Securities and Exchange Commission Terminology

This Appendix is an addition to and expansion of the terminology in Chapter 15 of the *Accounting Desk Book, Tenth Edition*. However, it is also more than in that includes not only "delegalized" terms that are fairly specific to the Securities and Exchange Comission and securities industry, but also terms more specific to the General Accounting Office as well as identification of several world-wide organizations with which these, and other U.S. government agencies deal.

Anticipated Transactions. Transactions an enterprise expects, but is not obligated, to carry out in the normal course of business. These are transactions other than those involving existing assets or liabilities or those necessitated by existing firm commitments.

Arm's Length Transaction. Transaction conducted as though the parties were unrelated to avoid any semblance of conflict of interest. For example, parents may rent real estate to their children under current law and still claim business deduction such as depreciation as long as the parents charge their children what they would charge someone who was not related.

Ask. The lowest price a broker asks customers to pay for a security.

Assets. Probable future economic benefits obtained or controlled by a particular entity as a result of past transactions or events.

At-the-Market. An offering into an existing trading market other than at a fixed price or through the facilities of a national securities exchange or to a market-maker otherwise than on an exchange.

Bank for International Settlements (BIS). Established in 1930 in Basle, Switzerland, by Western European central banks. One function is to provide forum for cooperative efforts by central banks of major industrial countries.

Basle Accord. Internationally developed risk-based capital standards framework for banks. (Representatives of bank regulatory bodies from 12 BIS member countries adopted a framework for establishing minimum capital standards for internationally active banks. Each country was responsible for enacting framework into its national regulations.)

Basle Committee on Banking Supervision. Includes central bank and bank supervisory representatives from 12 leading industrial nations (Belgium, Canada, France, Germany, Italy, Japan, Luxembourg, the Netherlands, Sweden, Switzerland, the United Kingdom, and the United States). A forum for addressing international bank regulation issues. Meets under auspices of the Bank for International Settlements in Basle, Switzerland. (See above.)

Beneficial Owner. The true owner of a security which may, for convenience, be recorded under the name of a nominee.

Bid. The highest price a broker is willing to pay for a security.

Black-Scholes Option Pricing Model. Model developed by Fischer Black and Myron Scholes to gauge whether options contracts are fairly valued. The model incorporates such factors as the volatility of a security's return, the level of interest rates, the relationship of the underlying stock's price to the "strike price" of the option, and the time remaining until the option expires.

Blind Pool. Limited partnership that does not specify the properties the general partner plans to acquire. If, for example, a real estate partnership is offered in the form of a blind pool, investors can evaluate the project only by looking at the general partner's track record.

Bond. A certificate which is evidence of a debt in which the issuer promises to repay a specific amount of money to the bondholder, plus a certain amount of interest, within a fixed period of time.

Broker; Broker/Dealer. An entity in the business of buying and selling securities, for a commission, on behalf of other parties.

Call. Contract giving the holder the right to buy stock from the writer at a designated price within a designated time; and conversely obligating the writer to sell stock at a specified price within a designated time period. (See **Put** below). Also refers to provisions in bond contracts that allow issuers to buy back bonds prior to their stated maturity.

Cash Account. A type of account with a broker-dealer in which the customer agrees to pay the full amount due for the purchase of securities within a short period of time, usually five business days.

Class of Securities. A group of similar securities that give shareholders similar rights. Stocks and bonds are the two main classes. They are subdivided into different classes—mortgage bonds and debentures, common and preferred stock, Class A or Class B common stock. All are itemized on a company's balance sheet.

Closed-End Fund. A type of investment company whose securities are traded on the open market rather than being redeemed by the issuing company. (See below.)

Closed-End Investment Company. A corporation in the business of investing its funds in securities of other corporations for income and profit. Investors wishing to "cash out" of the investment company do so by selling their shares on the open market, as with any other stock.

Combination Plan. An award with two or more separate components, each of which is actually a separate grant. Compensation costs are measured and recognized for each grant.

Commission. The fee charged by a broker-dealer for services performed in buying or selling securities on behalf of a customer.

Commodity Derivative Instruments. To the extent such instruments are not derivative financial instruments, they include commodity futures, commodity forwards, commodity swaps, commodity options, and other commodity instruments with similar characteristics, that are reasonably possible to be settled in cash or with another financial instrument.

Commodity Futures Trading Commission (CFTC). Established in 1974 by Congress, succeeding the Commodities Exchange Act of 1936. It regulates all commodities traded in organized contract markets. Polices matters of information and disclosure, fair trading practices, registration of firms and individuals, and the protection of customer funds, record keeping, and the maintenance of orderly futures and options markets.

Comprehensive Income. A financial statement presentation of accounting changes, during a given period, in net assets that are nonownership related like translation gains and losses. (Currently, U.S. GAAP does not cover this concept; however, since the FASB is planning to incorporate it in a new derivatives and hedging accounting standard, they are planning to issue exposure drafts on both during 1996.)

Core Capital. Tier 1 capital. At a minimum, a bank's core capital (common stockholders' equity, certain types of preferred stock, and minority equity investments in subsidiaries) must be at least 4%. 8% of net positions in foreign exchange activities recommended by the Basle Accord.

Core Deposits. Normally defined as the sum of all transaction accounts, savings deposits, and time deposits of less than $100,000.

Credit Equivalent Amounts. Contract's replacement cost or market value plus an additional amount, called an add-on, to reflect potential future credit risk. Based on Basle Accord's current exposure method.

Credit Risk. Exposure to the possibility of loss resulting from a counterparty's failure to meet its financial obligations.

Cross Volatility. The prices of two assets, which are very volatile, measures the relationship of the two assets. Takes into account the correlation between price movements of the two assets.

Dealer. A person in the business of buying and selling securities for his or her own account; participant in derivatives market. The latter are usually large banks, securities firms, insurance companies, or their affiliates. As dealers, they earn income by meeting the demand for derivatives, and they can also use derivatives for the same purpose as end users. (See **End user** below).

Delta Value. Measure of the sensitivity of an option's price to changes in the price of the underlying contract.

Derivative Commodity Instruments. To the extent the following instruments are not derivative financial instruments, they would include commodity futures, commodity forwards, commodity swaps, commodity options, and other commodity instruments with similar characteristics that are reasonably possible to be settled in cash or with another financial instrument.

Derivative Financial Instruments. Futures, forwards, swaps, options, and other financial instruments with comparable characteristics.

Derivatives. General term used in reference to both derivative financial instruments and derivative commodity instruments (defined above). So named because they "derive" their return from other instruments to which they are linked. The market value of a derivatives contract is derived from a reference rate, index, or the value of an underlying asset. These underlying assets, rates, and indexes include stocks, bonds, commodities, interest rates, foreign currency exchange rates, and indexes that reflect the collective value of underlying financial products. In addition to the basic instruments, over 600 more sophisticated derivatives and derivative-like instruments have been developed. They include interest rate caps, interest rate floors, fixed rate commitments, variable rate loan commitments, commitments to purchase stocks and bonds, forward interest rate agreements, and interest rate collars.

Direct Participation Program. Program letting investors participate directly in the cash flow and tax benefits of the underlying investments. Such programs are usually organized as limited partnerships.

Discretionary Account. A type of account with a broker/dealer in which the investor authorizes the broker to buy and sell securities, selected by the broker, at a price, amount, and time the broker believes to be best.

Dividend. A payment by a corporation to its stockholders, usually representing a share in the company's earnings.

End user. Participant in derivatives markets. Firm that use derivatives to manage (hedge) their financial risks or to speculate. Included are financial institutions, commercial firms, mutual and pension funds, and some government entities. (See **Dealer** above).

Equity Security. Any stock or similar security; or any security convertible, with or without consideration, into such a security, or carrying any warrant or right to subscribe to or purchase such a security, or any such warrant or right. More succinctly, an ownership interest in a company, most often taking the form of corporate stock.

European Community (EC). Made up of Belgium, Denmark, France, Germany, Greece, Ireland, Italy, Luxembourg, the Netherlands, Portugal, Spain, and the United Kingdom.

Face Value. The amount of money which the issuer of a bond promises to repay to the bondholder on or before the maturity date.

Fair Value. The amount at which a financial instrument could be exchanged in a current transaction between willing parties, other than in a forced or liquidation sale. Sales or quoted market prices in active markets are, when available, the best evidence of fair market value. If there is not a public market for the asset being traded, an estimate of fair value is made based on the prices for similar assets. The present value of expected future cash flows using an assumed discount rate can be used to arrive at a price for the product that is agreeable to the parties involved in the transaction.

Financial Instrument. Cash, evidence of an ownership interest in an entity, or contract that:

1) imposes on one entity a contractual obligation to deliver cash or another financial instrument to a second entity or to exchange other financial instruments on potentially unfavorable terms with the second entity, and also
2) conveys to that second entity a contractual right to receive cash or another financial instrument from the first entity or to exchange other financial instruments on potentially favorable terms with the first entity.

Fixed Award. An award of stock-based employee compensation for which vesting is based only on the employee's continued service to the employer for a specific period of time, not upon performance of specific conditions.

Form 8-K. A report which is filed only when a reportable event occurs which may have a significant effect on the future of a company and on the value of its securities. Such events include a change in control of the registrant, acquisition or disposition of assets, bankruptcy or receivership, or other material event. Form 8-K must be filed not later than 15 days after the date on which the specified event occurs.

Form 10-K. The annual report to the SEC which covers substantially all of the information required in Form S-1. It is the official audited financial report and narrative which publicly owned companies must file showing assets, liabilities, equity revenues, expenses, etc. Form 10-K is due 90 days after a company's December 31 fiscal year, or by March 31 of each year.

Form 10-Q. A quarterly report containing *unaudited* financial statements covering information that is "material." If certain types of events occur during the period, they must be reported on the form. The 10-Q is due 45 days after the end of each of the first three fiscal quarters and gives investors an indication of the company's condition.

Forward-Looking Statement. One containing a projection of revenues, income, income losses, earnings, earnings loss per share, capital expenditures, dividends, capital structure or other financial items; plans and objectives for future operations; statement of future economic performance.

Forwards and Futures. Contractual obligations for the holder to buy or sell a specific amount of an underlying asset, reference rate, or index at a specified price on a specified date.

Functional Currency. The currency of the primary economic environment in which the entity operates; normally, that is the currency of the environment in which an entity primarily generates and expends cash.

Grant Date. The date on which a stock-based compensation award is agreed to by an employer and employee. Employees who fulfill vesting requirements are entitled to issues of equity instruments or transfer of assets as of the grant date. Awards requiring shareholder approval are not considered granted until approval is obtained unless this is a mere formality.

Group of Ten, The. Eleven major industrial member countries that coordinate monetary and fiscal policies through general agreements to borrow, and other activities. Members are Belgium, Canada, France, Germany, Italy, Japan, the Netherlands, Sweden, Switzerland, the United Kingdom, and the United States.

Group of Thirty, The. An international financial policy organization whose members include representatives of central banks, international banks and securities firms, and academia.

Hedging. Traditionally, a strategy of entering into transactions of financial positions with primary purpose and effect being to protect an entity from exposure to interest rate, foreign exchange, or commodity price risk. Currently also considered to include "other risk adjusting activities" to adjust the level of risk, either up or down, but not necessarily to reduce it.

Historical Cost. The amount of cash, or its equivalent, originally paid to acquire an asset or in the case of a liability, proceeds in cash or its equivalent when the obligation was incurred.

Interest. The payment a corporate or governmental issuer makes to bondholders in return for the loan of money.

Interest Rate Risk. Risk of potential loss arising from changes in interest rates. One of the primary types of market risk banks face.

International Organization of Securities Commissions (IOSCO). In 1993, it included securities administrators from 63 countries. It facilitates efforts to coordinate international securities regulation.

International Swaps and Derivatives Association (ISDA). A trade association that represents more that 150 leading financial institutions worldwide. Membership includes investment, commercial, and merchant banks that deal in privately negotiated OTC derivatives transactions.

Intrinsic Value. The value of the underlying stock for which an option can be exercised. An option to buy a stock with an exercise price of $10 per share that is currently selling for $12 per share has an intrinsic value of $2 per share.

Issuance of an Equity Instrument. A company will issue an equity instrument when the seller and buyer have agreed upon the price. The instrument can be paid for with cash, an enforceable right to receive cash, another financial instrument, goods, or services. An equity instrument can be conditionally transferred to another party that permits the receiving party to subsequently choose whether or not to pay the consideration agreed upon, or to forfeit the right to the conditionally transferred instrument.

Legal Risk. Exposure to financial loss arising from adverse legal or regulatory body action.

Liability. Probable future sacrifice of economic benefit arising from the present obligation of a particular entity to transfer assets or provide services to other entities in the future as a result of past transactions or events.

Margin Account. A type of account with a broker/dealer, in which the broker agrees to lend the customer part of the amount due for the purchase of securities.

Market Risk. The risk of loss arising from adverse changes in market rates and prices, such as interest rates, foreign currency exchange rates, commodity prices, and similar market rate or price changes (e.g., equity prices).

Market Risk Sensitive Instruments. Derivative financial instruments, other financial instruments, and derivative commodity instruments, collectively.

Market Value Accounting. Based on the concept of fair value which has been defined as the price that could be obtained in an arm's length transaction between willing parties in other than a forced or liquidation sale. Values of assets and liabilities are increased or reduced as their estimated market value changes. Assigned market value will vary depending on factors such as fluctuation in interest rates and changes in credit quality.

Material Associated Person. Has a relationship to a broker/dealer to such a degree that its business activities are reasonably likely to have a material impact on the financial and operational condition of the broker/dealer. Figure in risk assessment of firm's derivatives risk management.

Measurement Date. The date at which the stock price that enters into measurement of the fair value of an award of employee stock-based compensation is fixed.

Minimum Value. An estimate of an option price which does not consider the expected volatility of the underlying stock. May be computed using a standard option-pricing model using a volatility of effectively zero. Also can be computed as the current price of the stock reduced to exclude the present value of any expected dividends during the option's life minus the present value of the exercise price.

Model. Types used may include variance/covariance, historical simulation, Monte Carlo simulation.

Money Market Fund. Generally, a mutual fund which typically invests in short-term debt instruments such as government securities, commercial paper, and large denomination certificates of deposits of banks.

Mutual Fund. Not legal terminology. It is a financial term commonly used in street jargon to mean an open-end investment company (see **Open-End Investment Company** below) as defined in the Investment Company Act of 1940. A pool of stocks, bonds, or other securities purchased by a group of investors and managed by a professional, registered investment company. The investment company itself is also commonly referred to as a mutual fund.

NASDAQ. National Association of Securities Dealers Automated Quotation System provides broker/dealers with bid and ask prices for some securities traded over-the-counter.

Net Asset Value. The dollar value of one share of a mutual fund at a given point in time, which is calculated by adding up the value of all of the fund's holdings and dividing by the number of outstanding shares.

Netting. Arriving at the difference between additions and subtractions or plus amounts and minus amounts.

No-Load Fund. A type of mutual fund that offers its shares directly to the public at their net asset value with no accompanying sales charge.

Nonpublic Entity. An entity that is not traded either on a stock exchange or in the over-the-counter market. A nonpublic entity will not have made a filing with a regulatory agency for public sale of any class of equity securities in a public market, nor is it an entity that is controlled by an entity that is bought and sold in a public market.

Nonvested Stock. Shares of stock that cannot be sold because the employee for whom the shares were granted has not yet fulfilled the vesting requirements to earn the right to the shares. The restriction against selling is necessary because the shares may be forfeited.

Notional Value. Reflects the total of underlying valuations. It is not necessarily a valid measure of risk for at least three reasons:

1) It does not account for offsetting exposures,
2) It does not consider differences in duration of contracts, and, thus, may not take into account varying sensitivity to interest rate fluctuation, and
3) It fails to take into consideration the various risk profiles of different types of derivatives and their underlying assets.

Odd Lot. Fewer than 100 shares of stock.

Open-End Investment Company or Fund. A corporation in the business of investing its funds in securities of other corporations for income and profit. An open-end company continuously offers new shares for sales and redeems shares previously issued to investors who want to cash out.

Operational Risk. Exposure to financial loss from inadequate systems, management failure, faulty controls, fraud, or human error.

Option. The contractual privilege (either customized and privately negotiated or standardized) of purchasing a specified quantity of a commodity or financial asset (Call) for a specified price, or delivering a specified quantity of a commodity or financial asset (Put) at a specified price (exercise price) on or before a future date. The contract grants the purchaser the right, but not the obligation, to buy or sell at the stated price within a specified period. A European-style option can only be exercised on its expiration date.

Organization for Economic Cooperation and Development (OECD). This organization has members from 24 developed countries. Its goals are to achieve high economic growth, contribute to sound economic expansion, and contribute to the expansion of world trade.

Other Financial Instruments. Loans, investments, structured notes, mortgage-backed securities, indexed debt instruments, interest-only and principal-only obligations, deposits, and other debt obligations. (In the SEC's proposals for amendments regarding derivative accounting policy disclosure, trade accounts receivable and trade accounts payable are not considered other financial instruments when their carrying amounts approximate fair value.) Examples of other financial instruments with characteristics similar to option contracts include interest rate caps or floors and fixed-rate loan commitments. Those instruments have characteristics similar to options because they have the potential for taking advantage of favorable movements in the price of an underlying asset or index with relatively little chance of loss from unfavorable price movements.

Over-the-Counter (OTC). A market for buying and selling stock between broker/dealers over the telephone rather than by going through a stock exchange.

Penny Stock. Stock that typically sells for less than $1 per share, although it may rise to as much as $10 per share after the initial public offering, usually because of heavy promotion. Penny stocks are usually offered by companies with a short, erratic history of revenue and earnings. They are more volatile than those of large, well-established firms traded on a stock exchange. All are traded over-the-counter, often in a regional market like Denver or Salt Lake City.

Performance Award or Performance Condition. An award to an employee rendering service to his or her employer for a specified period of time, or the achievement of a specified performance level of the enterprise as a whole or to some part of the enterprise such as a division. These are the "performance" requirements for a stock-based employee vesting compensation award.

Primary Market Risk Exposures. This term refers to a) the following categories of market risk: interest rate risk, foreign currency exchange rate risk, commodity price risk, and other similar market rate or price risks (e.g., equity prices); and, b) within each of these categories, the particular markets that present the primary risks of loss to the registrant.

For example, if an entity has a material exposure to foreign currency exchange rate risk, and is most vulnerable to changes in, say, dollar/yen, dollar/pound, and/or dollar/peso exchange rates within this category of market risk, the specific exposures should be disclosed.

Principal Stockholder. A person who a) owns 10% or more of an entity's common stock; b) can directly or indirectly control the entity; and c) can significantly influence the management and/or operations of the entity.

Prospectus. Document consisting of Part One of the registration statement filed with the SEC by the issuing corporation that must be delivered to all purchasers of newly issued securities. Provides detailed information about the company issuing the securities and about that particular offering.

Public Entity. Any entity that a) has its equity securities for sale or purchase on a foreign or domestic stock exchange, or in the over-the-counter market; b) has made a filing with a regulatory agency for the sale of any class of equity securities; and c) is controlled by an entity that is traded on a stock exchange or over-the-counter market, or, if not so traded, is controlled by an entity that is traded in a public market.

Public Float. The aggregate market value of the outstanding securities held by nonaffiliates.

Put. A contract giving the holder the right to sell stock to the writer at a designated price within a designated time; and conversely obligating the writer to buy stock at a specified price within a designated time period. (See **Option** above.)

Qualitative Disclosure. In general, disclosure that reveals important factors that cannot be precisely measured. Concerned with such information as experience, general caliber of management, employee morale, or status of labor relations rather than actual financial data about a company.

Quantitative Disclosure. Disclosure dealing with measurable factors such as value of assets, cost of capital, etc.

Quotation (Quote). The price at which a security may be bought or sold at any given time.

Reasonably Possible. The chance of a future transaction or event occurring is more than remote but less than probable.

Registered Securities. Stocks or bonds or other securities for which a registration statement has been filed with the SEC.

REIT. Real Estate Investment Trust, a type of company in which investors pool their funds to buy and manage real estate or to finance construction or purchases.

Reload Option/Option Granted with Reload Feature. Whenever an employee obtains grants for additional options, the reload option feature enables the employee to obtain automatic grants of additional options, using the shares of stock acquired by exercising the previously held options for shares, rather than cash, to cover the exercise price. The number of shares tendered determines the number of reload options granted. The market price of the stock on which the reload option is granted is the exercise price of the reload option.

Restricted Stock. "Restricted" is the term applied to fully-vested and outstanding stock for which the sale is restricted, either by government or by contract, for a specified period of time. Most stock grants to employees are better termed "nonvested" stock because they are "restricted" only to the extent that the shares may be forfeited before the employee fulfills the service or performance requirements; therefore, they are not fully vested.

Round Lot. Generally, one hundred shares of stock or multiples of 100.

Sensitivity Analysis. A general class of models that assesses the risk of loss in market risk sensitive instruments based on hypothetical changes in market rates or prices. The term sensitivity analysis does not refer to any one model for quantifying market risk.

Service Period. The specified time that the employee is obligated to perform the specified service in exchange for stock options or similar awards. If a specified earlier or shorter period is not defined, the vesting period is considered to be the service period.

Shelf Registration. Term used for Securities and Exchange Commission Rule 415, adopted in the 1980s, which allows a corporation to comply with registration requirements up to two years prior to a public offering of securities. With the registration on the shelf, the corporation, by simply updating regularly filed annual, quarterly, and related reports to the SEC, can go to the market as conditions become favorable, with a minimum of administrative preparation. The flexibility that corporate issuers gain results in substantial savings in money and time.

Significant Investee. An investee is "significant" if his or her investment exceeds 20% of the registrant's total assets or the investee provides more than 20% of the registrant's income.

Small Business Issuer. An entity that a) has revenues of less than $25,000,000; b) is a U.S. or Canadian issuer; c) is not an investment company; or d) if a majority-owned subsidiary, the parent corporation is also a small business issuer.

An entity is not a small business issuer, however, if it has a public float (the aggregate market value of the outstanding securities held by nonaffiliates) of $25,000,000 or more.

Soft Assets. May include intellectual property, research and development software, human capital, patents, copyrights, and brand names in contrast to traditional industrial assets such as plant, equipment, and real property.

Specialist. A member of a stock exchange who operates on the trading floor buying and selling shares of particular securities as necessary to maintain a fair and orderly market.

Stock-Based Compensation Plan. A compensation agreement that enables employees to receive shares of stock, stock options, or other equity instruments, or is an agreement that assumes an obligation to the employee in amounts that are based on the price of the employer's stock.

Stock Option. The holder has the right, but not the obligation, for a definite period of time, to buy or sell a specified number of shares of stock in the future at a price determined at the time the options are bought or sold.

Street Name. A name other than that of the beneficial owner (e.g., a broker/dealer) in which stock may be recorded, usually to facilitate resale.

Substantive Terms. A feature of a stock-based compensation plan for which the terms of the plan are understood by the employer and by the employee who is awarded the stock-based plan.

Supplementary Capital. Tier 2 capital.

Swaps. Agreements between counter parties to make periodic payments to each other for a specified period. In a simple interest rate swap, one party makes payments based on a fixed interest rate, while the counter party makes payments based on a variable rate. The contractual payments are based on a notional amount that for interest rate swaps is never actually exchanged.

Synthetic Instruments. Created by linking two or more distinct instruments whose collective characteristics resemble those of a prototype instrument. Example: interest rate swaps.

Takedown. Each participating investment banker's proportionate share of the securities to be distributed in a new or secondary offering. Removal of securities from the "shelf" in a shelf registration.

Tandem Plan. Two or more parts of a plan that has been awarded in which the exercise of one part cancels the other part(s) of the plan.

Time Value. The portion of the fair value (defined above) of an option that exceeds its intrinsic value (defined above). For example, if an option with an exercise buying price of $15 on a stock is currently selling for $20, the intrinsic value is $5. If the fair value of the option is $7, the time value is $2 ($7-$5=$2).

Trading Purposes. Debt and equity securities obtained for the purpose of gaining a quick profit from selling at a change in the market price rather than holding them for a longer period to realize gain from capital appreciation. Worth is stated at fair value in the financial statement.

Unit Investment Trust. A type of investment company with a fixed unmanaged portfolio, typically invested in bonds or other debt securities in which the interests are redeemable.

Value at Risk. A general class of models that makes possible an estimation of the risk of loss in market risk sensitive instruments. The term value at risk does not refer to any specific model for quantifying market risk. Value at risk models can be adapted to nontrading activities as well as to trading activities and to nonfinancial institutions as well as to financial institutions, depending on the model and assumptions selected by the particular entity.

Vest, Vested. An employee stock option that has become vested can normally be exercised immediately if the employee so desires. The award of a stock-based compensation plan becomes vested on the date that the employee's right to exercise the options' award is no longer a function of the employee meeting a specified service or performance condition of the employer.

Volatility. Measure of rapid or wide fluctuations of stock prices over a specified period of time in the past, which is termed historic volatility, or is expected to fluctuate in the future over a specified period of time, termed expected volatility. Normally expressed in annualized terms that are comparable regardless of the time segment considered—daily, weekly, or monthly price observations.

World Bank, The. Also referred to as International Bank for Reconstruction and Development. It was established in 1945, and is owned by 160 countries. Its objective is to raise the standard of living in developing countries by channeling financial resources to them from developed countries. It finances lending operations primarily from borrowing in international capital markets.

Yield. Generally, the return on an investment in a stock or bond, calculated as a percentage of the amount invested.

Appendix B
Interest Netting

The tax law requires that taxpayers who underpay their taxes must pay interest to the government for the period of underpayment. The IRS has limited authority to abate the interest that is required by statute. The Code generally requires the government to pay interest to taxpayers with respect to any overpayment of taxes. There are, however, a number of limitations on the government's liability for interest, including the rule that no interest is payable with respect to a tax refund claimed for a current year if the refund is issued within 45 days of the last day prescribed for filing a return claiming the refund.

THE INTEREST RATE

Prior to enactment of the Tax Reform Act of 1986, the same interest rate applied to underpayment and overpayments. The Act, however, provided for the interest rate charged on underpayment to be one percentage point higher than the interest rate paid on overpayments. The Omnibus Budget Reconciliation Act of 1990 added that, under certain conditions, the interest rate on large corporate underpayment would be three percentage points higher than the interest rate on overpayments. The differential between large corporate underpayment and certain corporate overpayments was increased in 1984 to 4.5 percentage points.

If an overpayment is credited against an underpayment, the effect of interest rate differences is reduced. If any portion of a tax is satisfied by credit of an overpayment, no interest will be imposed on the portion of the tax that is satisfied for any period during which, if the credit had not been made, interest would have been allowable with respect to such overpayment. The Code provides authority for the IRS to credit an overpayment against an underpayment.

ANNUAL INTEREST NETTING

Congress has recognized the potential burden that the interest rate differential places on taxpayers who have both overpayments and underpayment. Each time Congress has increased the interest rate differential, Congress has stated in legislative history that the IRS should implement the most comprehensive procedures consistent with sound administrative practice to allow overpayments to be credited against underpayment. The IRS has developed substantial crediting procedures to implement *interest netting*. The IRS will consider all increases and decreases in a taxpayer's liabilities within a single tax year before applying the statutory interest rules to that year. A taxpayer will not be charged the differential interest rate on an underpayment that is satisfied by credit of an overpayment arising in the same taxable year. The interest netting procedure is referred to as *annual interest netting*. Crediting is permitted for overpayments against underpayment for the period of time when the underpayment and overpayments are both unpaid and outstanding, even if they are from different tax years or for different types of tax. This procedure for interest netting is referred to as *offsetting*.

GLOBAL NETTING

The IRS generally does not net interest when a taxpayer realizes an overpayment in one tax year that overlaps with a deficiency that a taxpayer has already paid for a different tax year. Also, interest is not netted when an unpaid deficiency in one tax year overlaps with an overpayment that the IRS has already paid for a different tax year. This kind of interest netting is referred to as *global interest netting*. Global interest netting would allow a taxpayer or the IRS to recalculate interest for a certain period of time—whenever a taxpayer has either a new overpayment that overlaps with an underpayment that the taxpayer has already paid, or to a new underpayment that overlaps with an overpayment that the IRS has already paid to the taxpayer.

PROBLEMS

Global netting has caused various problems, so the IRS has now asked for public comments on the following matters:

1) In view of the policy generally favoring the finality of tax determinations, should a rule concerning the finality of global interest netting com-

putations be adopted, and, if so, what should the rule be? What effect, if any, should the statute of limitations have on global interest netting, particularly the language in the current rules regarding the applicable period of limitations? Should the statute of limitations be kept open longer in light of global interest netting?

2) When would it be appropriate for the IRS to net interest globally, for a particular tax year or period? Would it be appropriate to net interest globally, before the final decision of an appeal or court decision for a tax period overlapping with the period at issue, that might affect the interest calculation for such period? Would it be appropriate to net interest globally, before the final decision of an appeal or court decision for a tax period that does not overlap with the period at issue, if such decision could produce an adjustment, such as a net operating loss or credit, that might affect the interest calculation for such period?

3) What would be the effect of carrybacks and carryforwards, e.g; net operating losses, and various credits, on the global interest for such period? Or should global interest netting calculations only be made after carryforwards and carrybacks that might affect the period at issue are finally determined?

4) Does global interest netting present any unique implications for taxpayers filing consolidated returns?

5) How would global interest netting interact with other U.S. international tax provisions?

IRS Computer Problems

The government's computer system does not have the data storage capacity to keep information concerning paid deficiencies and paid refunds on line. The IRS cannot make global interest netting calculations on its computer system, but must instead retrieve the data on paid deficiencies and paid refunds from its computer storage files and then manually make the interest calculations. This procedure could entail a significant additional commitment of IRS resources, primarily because of the need to verify the accuracy and completeness of the data necessary to make a global interest netting calculation and ensure an accurate calculation.

To the extent that taxpayers or practitioners currently make global interest netting calculations for themselves or their clients, the IRS would like to receive detailed descriptions of how those calculations are performed, the cost of performing those calculations, and the reasons why the method used by particular taxpayers or practitioners would be appropriate to apply to large numbers of taxpayers without requiring significant additional government resources. How should the IRS fulfill its obligation to verify the accuracy and completeness of all taxpayer data relevant to make a global interest netting calculation for a particular period given the computer data storage limitations?

Appendix C
Lobbying Expense

The following discussion covers the tax rules that define influencing legislation for purposes of the deduction disallowance for certain amounts paid or incurred in connection with influencing legislation. These rules include the changes made in IRS regulations by the Omnibus Budget Reconciliation Act of 1993, and will assist business and certain tax-exempt organizations in complying with the Internal Revenue Code. (The new rules were effective July 21, 1995.) The new rules describe the costs that are properly allocable to lobbying activities and permit taxpayers to use any reasonable method to allocate those costs between lobbying activities and other activities. A method is not reasonable unless it is applied consistently, allocates a proper amount of costs, including labor and general administrative costs, to lobbying activities, and is consistent with certain special rules of the regulations. The regulations provide that a taxpayer can use the following methods of allocating costs to lobbying activities:

1) The ratio method.
2) The gross-up method.
3) An allocation method that applies the principles of section 263A and the regulations thereunder of the Internal Revenue Code.
4) Any other reasonable method.

THE RATIO AND GROSS-UP METHODS

Under the *ratio method*, a taxpayer multiplies the total costs of operations, excluding third-party costs, by a fraction. That fraction is arrived at by using the taxpayer's lobbying hours as the numerator and the total labor hours as the denominator. The taxpayer then adds the result to its third-party costs to allocate its costs to lobbying activities. (This regulation considers *total costs of operations* to be the total costs of the taxpayer's trade or business for a taxable year, excluding third-party costs.)

Under the *gross-up method*, a taxpayer allocates costs to lobbying activities by multiplying the taxpayer's basic labor costs for lobbying hours by 175%. For this purpose, the taxpayer's basic labor costs are limited to wages or other similar costs of labor, such as guaranteed payment for services. For example, pension costs and other employee benefits are not included in basic labor costs. As with the ratio method, third party costs are then added to the result of the calculation to arrive at the total costs to allocate to lobbying activities.

Although the gross-up method provides a simple way to calculate costs allocated to lobbying activities, it does not simplify record keeping because taxpayers have to keep track of the lobbying labor hours of clerical and support staff in order to determine lobbying labor costs.

To combat this problem, the regulations provide an alternative gross-up method. Taxpayers can treat as zero the lobbying labor hours of personnel who engage in secretarial, clerical, support, and other administrative activities that do not involve significant judgment with respect to the lobbying activity. However, if a taxpayer uses this alternative, costs for lobbying labor hours must be multiplied by 225%. The gross-up factors, including the 225% factor, are intended to approximate the average gross-up factors for all taxpayers. If the regulations provided gross-up factors tailored to various trades, business or industries, the gross-up method would no longer be a simplified method. Taxpayers who do not consider either of these methods or the allocation method appropriate for them may use any *reasonable* method of allocating costs to lobbying activities.

The regulations provide that taxpayers who do not pay or incur reasonable labor costs for their personnel engaged in lobbying activities may use the ratio method, but not the gross-up method. On the other hand, tax-exempt organizations affected by the lobbying disallowance rules may use the gross-up method or the ratio method even if some of their lobbying activities are conducted by volunteers. Because volunteers are not taxpayers' personnel, time spent by volunteers is excluded from the taxpayer's lobbying labor hours and total labor hours.

Taxpayers who use the ratio method or the gross-up method must account for certain third-party costs. The regulations define third-party costs as amounts paid or incurred for lobbying activities conducted by third parties, such as amounts paid to lobbyists and dues that are allocable to lobbying expenditures, and amounts paid or incurred for travel and entertainment that relate to lobbying activities. If the third-party cost is allocable only partially to lobbying activities, only that portion of the cost must be allocated to lobbying activities under both the ratio method and the gross-up method.

Labor hours spent by personnel for a small period of time on lobbying activities can treat time spent by personnel as zero, if the time is less than 5% of the person's time, except this rule does not apply to direct contact lobbying with legislators and covered executive branch officials.

DIRECT CONTACT LOBBYING

All hours spent by a person on direct contact lobbying, as well as the hours that a person spends in connection with direct contact lobbying, including traveling, must be allocated to lobbying activities. For this purpose, an activity is direct contact lobbying and qualifies as a lobbying activity if it is a meeting, telephone conversation, letter, or other similar means of communication with a legislator, or other covered official executive. Direct contact applies only to the individuals who make the direct contact, not to support personnel who engage in research, preparation, and other background activities that do not involve a direct contact.

A lobbying communication is any communication that:

1) Refers to specific legislation and reflects a view on that legislation, or
2) Clarifies, amplifies, modifies, or provides support for views reflected in a prior lobbying communication.

The term specific legislation includes both legislation that has not yet been introduced in a legislative body, and a specific legislative proposal that the taxpayer either supports or opposes. A taxpayer can be considered to have reflected a view on specific legislation even without specifically stating that he or she supports or opposes that legislation. Moreover, a taxpayer's balanced or technical analysis of legislation reflects a view on some aspect of the legislation and, therefore, is a lobbying communication.

Whether a communication refers to a specific legislative proposal can vary with a proposal. Although the regulation does not actually define the term *special legislative proposal*, it does provide some guidance. It suggests that an attempt to influence legislation means a lobbying communication and all activities such as research, preparation, and other background activities are engaged in for the purpose of making or supporting a lobbying communication. The purpose or purposes for engaging in an activity are determined based on all the facts and circumstances. If a taxpayer engages in an activity for a lobbying purpose, and for some nonlobbying purpose, the taxpayer must treat the activity as engaged in according to the multipurpose rule—partially for a lobbying purpose and partially for a nonlobbying purpose

Reasonable Costs

The regulations do not specify methods for accomplishing a *reasonable cost* allocation in the case of multiple purpose activities. The regulations do specify two methods that may *not* be appropriate. A taxpayer's treatment of multiple purpose activities will, in general, not result in a reasonable allocation if it allocates to influencing legislation:

1) Only the incremental amount of costs that would not have been incurred but for the lobbying purpose.
2) An amount based on the number of purposes for engaging in that activity without regard to the relative importance of those purposes.

The regulations are clarified to treat allocations based solely upon the number of purposes for engaging in an activity as not reasonable. This approach is intended to indicate that an allocation based on the number of purposes may be reasonable if it reflects the relative importance of various purposes, even if the allocation is not precise. For example, if a taxpayer engages in an activity for two purposes of substantially similar importance, treating the activity as engaged in 50% for each purpose is reasonable.

The regulations provide special rules for activities engaged in for a lobbying purpose where the taxpayer later concludes that no lobby communication will be made regarding that activity. Specifically, these activities should be treated as if they had not been engaged in for a lobbying purpose if, as of the taxpayer's timely filed return, the taxpayer no longer expects, under any reasonably foreseeable circumstances, that a lobbying communication will be made that is supported by the activity. Therefore, the taxpayer need not treat any amount allocated to that activity for that year as an amount to which the regulation applies. If the taxpayer should reach that conclusion at any time after the filing date, then the amount not previously satisfying the rules allocated to that activity is treated as an amount that is paid or incurred only at that time. In effect the taxpayer is treated as if he or she incurred the costs relating to that activity in that later year in connection with a nonlobbying activity. A special rule is provided for exempt organizations which permits those organizations to instead treat these amounts as reducing, but not below zero, their expenditures beginning with that year and continuing for subsequent years to the extent not treated in prior years as reducing those expenditures.

Special Rules for Paid Volunteers

A special rule covers so-called *paid volunteers*. If for the purpose of making or supporting a lobbying communication, one taxpayer uses the services or facilities of a second taxpayer and does not compensate the second taxpayer for the full cost of the services or facilities, the purpose and actions of the first tax-payer are imputed to the second taxpayer. For example, if a trade association uses the services of a member's employee, at no cost to the association, to conduct research or similar activities to support the trade association's lobbying communication, the trade association's purpose and action are imputed to the member. As a result, the member is treated as influencing legislation with respect to the employee's work in support of the trade association's lobbying communication. This rule for special imputation is intended to deny a deduction for the amounts paid or incurred by a taxpayer participating in a group activity involving a lobbying purpose and a lobbying communication, even if the lobbying communication was made by a person other than the taxpayer.

INFLUENCING LEGISLATION

The statutory terminology *influencing legislation* includes lobbying communications with government employees or officials who may participate in the formulation of legislation. No exceptions are intended other than for communications pursuant to subpoena or similar compulsion. Participating with a federal advisory committee is influencing legislation if the purpose of the participant's activities is to make or support a lobbying communication, even if the lobbying communication is made by another participant, or by the federal advisory committee as a whole.

Appendix D
Tip Income

This discussion concerns how tip income is taxed and how to report it to the IRS on the federal income tax return. The employees of food and beverage companies are the main subjects of this review; the record keeping rules and other information also apply to other workers who receive tips, e.g, hairdressers, cab drivers, casino dealers.

All tips received by employees are taxable income and are subject to federal income taxes. They must include in gross income all tips received directly from customers and tips from charge customers that are paid to the employer who must pay them to the employee. In addition, cash tips of $20 or more that an employee receives in a month while working for any one employer are subject to withholding of income tax, Social Security retirement tax, and Medicare tax. The employee should report tips to the employer in order to determine the correct amount of these taxes.

Tips and other pay are used to determine the amount of Social Security benefits that an employee or survivor receives when he or she retires, becomes disabled, or dies. Noncash tips are not counted as wages for Social Security purposes. Future Social Security Administration (SSA) benefits can be figured correctly only if the SSA has the correct information. To make sure that an employee has received credit for all his or her earnings, the employee should request a statement of earnings from the SSA at least every other year. The SSA will send the person a statement that should be carefully checked to be sure it includes all of the employee's earnings.

Every large food and beverage business must report to the IRS any tips allocated to the employees. Generally, tips must be allocated to be paid by employees when the total tips reported to an employer by employees are less than 8% of the establishment's food and beverage sales by that employee. This necessitates the employer and employees keeping accurate records of the employees' tip income.

DAILY RECORD OF TIPS

An employee must keep a daily record or other documentation to prove the amount of tip income reported on the tax return. The daily record must show the employee's name and address, the employer's name, and the name of the establishment where the employee works. The daily record must show the amount of cash tips received directly from customers or from other employees, tips from credit card charge customers when paid to the employee by the employer, the amount of tips paid out to other employees through tip-split or other tip-sharing arrangements, and the names of the other employees to whom an employee has paid tips. The daily record should show the entries on or near the date the tip income is received. The record should also show the date each entry to the record is made. If a daily record is not kept, other documentation of the tip income received must be maintained.

Other documentation must be as credible and reliable as a daily record; it must show the tips added to checks by customers and paid over to the employee, or the amounts paid for food and beverages for which the employee usually would receive a tip. Other documentary records, copies of which should be kept, are restaurant bills, credit card charges, and charges under any other arrangement containing amounts added by customers as tips. If an employee fails to report tips to the employer as required, the employee can be subject to a penalty equal to 50% of the employee's Social Security requirement tax and Medicare tax, in addition to the tax that is owed.

EMPLOYER RECORDS FOR TIP ALLOCATION

Large food and beverage establishments are required to report certain additional information about tips to the IRS. To make sure that employees are reporting tips correctly, employers must keep records to verify amounts reported by employees. Certain employers must allocate tips if the percentage of tips reported by employees falls below a required minimum percentage of gross sales. To allocate tips means to assign an additional amount as tips to each employee whose reported tips are below the required percentage. The rules apply to premises where:

1) Food and beverages are provided for consumption on the premises.

2) Tipping is customary.
3) The employer normally employed more than 10 people on a typical business day during the preceding calendar year.

Tip allocation rules do not apply to food and beverage establishments where tipping is not customary, such as:

1) A cafeteria or fast food restaurant.
2) A restaurant that adds a service charge of 10% or more to 95% or more of its food and beverage sales.
3) Food and beverage establishments located outside the United States.

The rules apply only if the total amount of tips reported by all tipped employees to the employer is generally less than 8% of the establishment's total food or beverage sales. If reported tips total less than 8% of total sales, the employer must allocate the difference between 8% of total sales and the amount of reported tips among all tipped employees. The employer is to exclude carryout sales, state and local taxes, and sales with a service charge of 10% or more when figuring total sales.

Usually, the employer will allocate to all affected employees their share of allocated tips every payroll period. However, the employer should not withhold any taxes from the allocated amount. No allocation will be made to the employee if he or she has reported tips at least 8% of his or her share of the establishment's total food and beverage sales.

ALLOCATION FORMULA

The allocation can be done either under a formula agreed to by both the employer and the employees or, if they cannot reach an agreement, under a formula prescribed by IRS regulations. The allocation formula in the regulations provides that tips allocations are made only to directly tipped employees. If tips are received directly from customers, the employees are directly tipped employees, even if the tips are turned over to a tip pool. Waiters, waitresses, and bartenders are usually considered directly tipped employees. If tips are normally received directly from customers, an employee is an indirectly tipped employee. Examples are busboys, service bartenders, and cooks. If an employee receives tips both directly and indirectly through tip splitting or tip pooling, the employee is treated as a directly tipped employee.

If customers of the establishment tip less than 8% on average, either the employee or a majority of the directly tipped employees can petition to have the allocation percentage reduced from 8%. This petition is made to the district director for the IRS district in which the establishment is located. The percentage cannot be reduced below 2%.

A user fee must be paid with the petition. A user fee is required to have the IRS consider a petition to lower the tip allocation percentage. The fee must be paid by check or money order made out to the Internal Revenue Service. The user fee amount for 1995 was $275; the district director in the taxpayer's area will know if this amount has changed.

The employees' petition to lower the allocation percentage must be in writing and must contain enough information to allow the district director to estimate with reasonable accuracy the establishment's actual tip rate. This information might include the changed tip rate, type of establishment, menu prices, location, hours of operation, amount of self-service required, and whether the customer receives the check from the server or pays the server for the meal. If the employer possesses any relevant information, the employer must provide it to the district upon request of the employees or the district director.

The employees' petition must be consented to by more than one-half of the directly tipped employees working for the establishment at the time the petition is filed. If the petition covers more than one establishment, it must be consented to by more than one-half of the total number of directly tipped employees of the covered establishments. The petition must state the total number of directly tipped employees of the establishment(s) and the number of directly tipped employees consenting to the petition.

The petition may cover two or more establishments if the employees have made a good faith determination that the tip wages are essentially the same and if the establishments are owned by the same employer; essentially the same type of business; and in the same Internal Revenue Service region.

A petition that covers two or more establishments must include the names and locations of the establishments and must be sent to the district director for the district in which the greatest number of covered establishments are located. If there is an equal number of covered establishments in two or more districts, the employees can choose which district to petition. Employees who file a petition must promptly notify their employer of the petition. The employer must then promptly furnish the district director with an annual information return form showing the tip income and allocated tips filed for the establishment for the three immediately preceding calendar years.

The employer will report the amount of tips allocated to employees on the employees' Form W-2 separately from wages and reported tips. The employer bases withholding only on wages and reported tips. The employer should not withhold income, Social Security, and Medicare taxes from the allocated amount. Any incorrectly withheld taxes should be refunded to the employee by the employer.

If an employee leaves a job before the end of the calendar year and requests an early Form W-2, the employer does not have to include a tip allocation on the Form W-2. However, the employer can show the actual allocated amount if it is known, or show an estimated allocation. In January of the next year, the employer must provide Form W-2 if the early Form W-2 showed no allocation and the employer later determined that an allocation was required, or if the estimated allocation shown was wrong by more than 5% of the actual allocation.

If an employee does not have adequate records for his or her actual tips, the employee must include the allocated tips shown on the Form W-2 as additional tip income on the tax return. If the employee has records, allocated tips should not be shown on the employee's return. Additional tip income is included only if those records show more tips received than the amount reported to the employer.

Appendix E
Proposed FASB Statements

DERIVATIVES AND HEDGING

Unless the Financial Accounting Standards Board runs into a storm of opposition as they did in connection with the standard for accounting for stock-based compensation (FASB 123), probably one of the upcoming Statements will be the eagerly awaited next step on the way to answering problems in dealing with derivatives. The understanding is that the Board plans to issue an Exposure Draft of a new derivatives and hedging accounting standard during the summer of 1996, hopefully in time for a finalized version of the new standard to be effective for 1997.

The proposal as now constituted would require all derivative financial instruments to be measured at fair value and recognized on the balance sheet as assets or liabilities. Derivative financial instruments could be designated as a hedge linked to one of three possible exposures:

1) A forecasted transaction.
2) An existing asset, liability, or firm commitment.
3) The foreign currency exposure of a net investment in a foreign entity.

A change in the fair value in each of these designations would be as follows:

1) A change in the fair value of a derivative instrument designated as a hedge of a forecasted transaction would be reported as a component of comprehensive income in the period of change, then recognized in

income on the date initially specified on which the forecasted transaction was scheduled to take place.

U.S. GAAP does not presently include a comprehensive income concept. The FASB plans to issue an Exposure Draft on this topic in anticipation of employing it in connection with this and possibly other future standards. Comprehensive income refers to a financial statement presentation of the accounting changes in equity (net assets) during a period from transactions and/or circumstances that are nonownership related, such as translation gains and losses. It includes all those changes in equity during the specific period except any resulting from owner investments or distributions to owners.

2) Change in the fair value of a derivative financial instrument designated as a hedge of an existing asset, liability, or firm commitment would be recognized in income in the period of change. The change in the period of the fair value of the asset, liability, or firm commitment being hedged would be recognized in earnings to the extent of offsetting changes in value of the hedging instrument. An adjustment would then be made to the carrying amount of the item being hedged.

3) The change in the fair value of a derivative financial instrument or a foreign currency-denominated cash instrument designated as a hedge of a foreign currency exposure of a net foreign investment would be reported in the same manner as the related translation adjustments. If a particular foreign currency is designated as a subsidiary's functional currency, the fair value change is recognized as a component of the period's comprehensive income. If the U.S. dollar is designated as a subsidiary's functional currency, the fair value change is recognized in income for the period. This treatment is consistent with FASB 52's existing accounting for hedges of net investments.

OTHER FASB STANDARDS IN THE MAKING

The FASB is planning to issue two other new standards in the next few months covering:

1) Consolidated financial statement policies and procedures.
2) Transfers of financial assets and extinguishments of liabilities.

The new consolidated statement standard will adopt the economic entity approach to consolidation and a control criterion for determining what entities are to be consolidated. The effect will be to include minority interest in owners' equity and a component of income, move many assets and liabilities currently treated as off-balance sheet items to balance sheet items, eliminate the recognition of profits in consolidated statements from sales of subsidiary company equity, and encourage multistage acquisition of 100% interests.

The FASB's anticipated transfer of financial assets and extinguishment of liabilities standard would require that transferred assets could be derecognized only when control is surrendered, rather than as required by the present standard when risks and rewards related to the asset are passed to another party. A liability would be extinguished under the new proposal when the creditor no longer has ultimate responsibility for the liability.

Note: The above anticipated standard was adopted by the FASB as *Transfer and Servicing of Financial Assets* and *Extinguishment of Liabilities,* FASB 125.

Index